The Emotionally Connected Classroom

To Shelley. Your passion for life, love, adventure, and spirited play knows no bounds.

The Emotionally Connected Classroom

Wellness and the Learning Experience

Bill Adair

FOR INFORMATION:

Corwin

A SAGE Company

2455 Teller Road

Thousand Oaks, California 91320

(800) 233-9936

www.corwin.com

SAGE Publications Ltd.

1 Oliver's Yard

55 City Road

London, EC1Y 1SP

United Kingdom

SAGE Publications India Pvt. Ltd.

B 1/I 1 Mohan Cooperative Industrial Area

Mathura Road, New Delhi 110 044

India

SAGE Publications Asia-Pacific Pte Ltd

18 Cross Street #10-10/11/12

China Square Central

Singapore 048423

Printed in the United States of America.

ISBN 978-1-5443-5636-5

Program Director: Jessica Allan

Content Development Editor: Lucas Schleicher

Senior Editorial Assistant: Mia Rodriguez

Production Editor: Tori Mirsadjadi

Copy Editor: Deanna Noga

Typesetter: Cenveo

Proofreader: Ellen Howard

Indexer: Amy Murphy

Cover Designer: Rose Storey

Marketing Manager: Margaret O'Connor

This book is printed on acid-free paper.

SUSTAINABLE FORESTRY INITIATIVE Certified Chain of Custody
At Least 10% Certified Forest Content
www.sfiprogram.org
SFI-01028

19 20 21 22 23 10 9 8 7 6 5 4 3 2 1

Contents

Acknowledgments

As a long-time high school teacher, it was becoming increasingly difficult to ignore an alarming change in my classroom. Anxious, stressed-out children were becoming the norm, and teaching the way I always had was no longer working. My well-intended labors often fell short and, on occasion, ended in frustration for myself and tears for my students. Sometimes it felt like children had little desire to challenge themselves and grow. Even stranger yet, it appeared many children had an aversion toward feeling good and adamantly denied healthy connected activities that should, under normal circumstances, be very pleasurable. This did not make sense.

As fate would have it, my long-time friend Todd Ritchey, a life coach and emotional addiction specialist, was experiencing great success with a new approach for clients challenged by a wide range of addictive behaviors. I began tinkering with his ideas in my classroom. It is hard to imagine, but a therapeutic model designed to break the chains of the most powerful substance or behavior addictions was a perfect fit for children "stuck" in a world of unhealthy emotions and thinking patterns. The immediate and profound outcomes were remarkable and set me on a new path for what "teaching" meant to me.

I have had the good fortune to learn from and work alongside many great teachers. They have all shaped my life's journey in the best way possible. I must acknowledge my favorite coaches and teachers. Bob Baldwin, Jack Schreiber, and Shoji Yamazaki provided the inspiration to shoot for the stars. You have all passed, but your lessons live on. Thank you to my amazing teaching colleagues. In many ways your everyday demonstrations of healthy connections, caring, and community building have filled the pages of this book.

Thank you to Rachel Armstrong for the idea to write a book, and for the many conversations that got it off to a start. Thank you to Frances Friend, Naomi McDonnell, and Lisa Dube for volunteering to be the first readers of the early drafts. Special thanks to my wife Shelley for being kind enough to share the truth. My attempts at a book about the emotional experience were "boring," and her advice and thoughts guided the infusion of Johnny, Inubu, and the stories that brought it to life.

Thank you to my wonderful family. My parents, Tom Adair and Evelyn Westover, provided a loving childhood filled with sport and opportunity. I am forever grateful for the unconditional support of my in-laws, Ron and Bev Kimak. Thank you to my inspirational children, Keegan, Karly, and Connor. I have learned much watching you grow, overcome challenge, and flourish. Finally, one last accolade for my wife, who took care of just about everything while I progressed with my incredibly slow typing.

Special thanks to the Corwin team and Program Director Jessica Allen for giving a new writer an opportunity to publish a book I hope will change the way readers think about wellness and the learning experience.

SPECIAL ACKNOWLEDGMENT: TODD RITCHEY

Emotional Addiction consultant for *The Emotionally Connected Classroom.*

Todd Ritchey is an addiction specialist with over 15 years of experience as an interventionist, life coach, and mentor. He has treated families and couples dealing with relationship challenges and substance, behavioral, and emotional addictions. Todd has generously shared his expertise and unique perspective for emotional healing in the classroom. He has coauthored two books with neuroscientist John Montgomery.

PUBLISHER'S ACKNOWLEDGMENTS

Corwin gratefully acknowledges the contributions of the following reviewers:

Abbey Duggins, PhD
Director of Curriculum and Instruction
Saluda County Schools
Saluda, SC

Leslie Goines
School Counselor
Massac County High School
Metropolis, IL

Leslie Hitchens, EdD
Middle School Supervisor
St. Paul Public Schools
Saint Paul, MN

Scott Mandel, PhD
Teacher, Staff Development Leader, Author
Los Angeles Unified School District
Pacoima, CA

Kathy Rhodes
Principal
Hinton Schools
Hinton, IA

Michelle Strom
Language Arts Teacher/Mentor
Lander Schools
Lander, WY

Bonnie Tryon, EdD
Mentor Coach, SAANYS Representative
New York State Education Department
Latham, NY

About the Author

Bill Adair earned his undergraduate degree and teacher's certificate at Simon Fraser University and his master's degree at San Diego State. His innovative teaching model was a response to growing anxiety, low resiliency, and motivational challenges in his classroom. Bill lives and teaches in Vancouver British Columbia. He enjoys presenting at workshops and conferences and passionately shares The Emotionally Connected Classroom model with university teacher training programs.

Prologue
Survival Mode

INUBU

The evening stars shone bright in the darkened sky, but they offered little useful light under the forest canopy and thick cover of brush. In any other circumstance, it would have been a beautiful night as the tribe shared stories and laughter around a dancing campfire. Tonight was different. Inubu was very frightened; he was alone in the wild. Few things were more dangerous. Only two moons ago one of the hunters did not return from his search for deer. He was an experienced and brave warrior. Inubu was only a boy.

He peered out the small opening of the unfamiliar cave and tried to recall how he could have gotten into so much trouble. His mind felt foggy, and it was difficult to think, but his thoughts slowly brought him back to the start of what had begun as a very special day.

He was playing hunters with his friends on the edge of the transient settlement. The boys knew not to travel far from the safety of the tribe, because dangerous animals were always a threat. At his side, he carried a simple but well-crafted bow his father had helped him make. It felt good in his small hands. He had learned how to use it by watching the older boys practice their skills for the upcoming hunts. One day, he hoped to join the real hunters and bring home food for his village. That would be a proud day.

He was surprised when his father told him that day was today. Inubu had been alive for only eleven seasons. That was young for a first hunt. His heart raced with excitement as the group of men left the safety of the small encampment. He wasn't really worried. After all, he was with father and his mother's brother—there were no stronger or braver tribesmen. His only true duty was to watch the group and stay close. Warnings to stay vigilant were clear. Together they were safe. Separation in the forest was another matter.

Thinking back, Inubu was angry with himself. In his excitement, his eyes drifted from his father to the thick brush. Maybe he would be the hunter to spot the prey. He had forgotten his first priority: keep watch and stay together. Consumed by exploring new lands and searching for animals he allowed himself to get distracted. He wasn't sure when he was separated; he only knew he had been alone for more than half the day. Desperately he tried to find his way back to the village, but with the setting sun, his plight had only worsened.

The cave was shallow but dry. It might offer protection from the rain, but a bear or large forest cat would have little difficulty pulling him out. His heart raced as he imagined teeth and claws dragging him helplessly from his shelter. His thoughts darkened as the blood soaked vision repeated itself over and over with ever-increasing severity and clarity. Would he fight bravely or give himself peacefully to the beast?

There were moments of reprieve in the quiet of the cave when safe feelings of home crept into his heart. They felt good, but fears continued to creep back and dominate his anxious thoughts. He was exhausted and considered trying to sleep the night away. He knew that would not happen. Frightened as he was, Inubu could only imagine the unfiltered terrors his unsettling dreams would create. Why had this happened to him?

The snap and crack of twigs suddenly shook Inubu from his stupor. A new energy raced through his body. His sleepy eyes widened, and his heart began to race. Something was moving closer to the cave. His body trembled as he clumsily reached for his bow. The sounds grew louder as a nearby bush began to shake. It was too dark to see, but he could tell the beast was large. He was about to die.

What could a boy possibly do? His father would fearlessly charge from the cave and slay the beast. He tried to gather the courage to do the same, but his terrified body told a different story, his muscles frozen in fear. The bush began to part. He lowered his eyes and helplessly accepted his fate. The tribe would not miss him.

JOHNNY

Rat-tat-tat-tat. The nearby gunfire echoed in his ears as his eyes carefully peaked across the hood of the burnt-out car. The debris and smoke of warfare made it difficult to see his enemies. He was surrounded and trapped. The sense of invincibility he felt when he entered the ruined city with six highly skilled squadron members by his side had long since left him. They were the closest friends he ever had. Two of them were already dead. He was sure he would be next. Running from his sheltered position would make that a certainty. Johnny hunkered down and hoped his allies would come to his aid. He was the best of the team and had rescued the others multiple times. "I hope they care enough."

THE EMOTIONALLY CONNECTED CLASSROOM

Johnny thought it was strange he wasn't that frightened. The truth was that he had never felt so alive. With his gun straddled across his chest, he felt safe and confident. He was really good at this. Here he had friends who respected him. At home he had never really experienced the same. He couldn't say that his parents didn't love him, but he knew they loved his older brother more. He was a star athlete and an excellent student. Johnny was neither. This was a better place for him.

"Johnny!" A call from the distance broke his concentration. It wasn't a squadron member. He put down his controller and left the game. It was time to go to school. His anxiety began to rise.

Introduction

Every child wants to belong.

Every child wants to contribute.

Every child wants to learn.

Children want to be their best.

These authentic truths liberate students from stereotypes and reputations that negatively define them. They inspire hope for teachers that there is something positive and beautiful to strive for within every child. Compassion and understanding open the door for new beginnings.

THE PURSUIT OF AUTHENTIC REWARD

All children want to be happy and experience a joyful life. Many just don't know what that looks like, where to find it, or how to embrace it as their own. Children want experiences that make them feel good, but all too often they find their endeavors emotionally muted and less than satisfying. A mountain of texts and tweets smothers warm encounters with those they love. Confusion and anxiety rise as media pressures to be someone they are not begin to dominate their thoughts. Ultrasafe environments created by loving but fearful parents limit purposeful challenge and learning. Isolating technological obsessions replace casual meetings and memories made with multiple friends at the park. The pressures of a disconnected inauthentic world have slowly eroded nature's plan for what it means to be a child.

In the absence of authentic healthy connections, attachments to unhealthy ones are almost a certainty.

For the child lacking authentic connections and feel-good rewards, an unhealthy emotional payoff is more attractive than no payoff at all. This opens the door to dysfunctional behaviors and beliefs that incite anger, guilt, shame, or feelings of "less than." The downward spiral continues as they bring their anxiety to school only to be tested, judged, and still meet expectations for optimal performance and learning. This can be a monumental task for a child more concerned about simply surviving an anxious existence.

> *At some point, a diagnosable mental health issue will emerge for about 25% of students.*
> (Merikangas, 2010)

Most experienced teachers willingly share their belief that the classroom is a much more challenging and complex environment than it once was. As the number of chronically dysfunctional or "identified" children on class lists soars, compassion collides with stress as overwhelmed teachers struggle to meet the diverse needs and emotional challenges of their students. An ultra-competitive, curriculum-driven education model separating children into winners and losers exacerbates the scenario. For teachers, falling short is a painful experience. Making choices of whom to leave behind is not an option.

EMOTIONS: THE CREATOR OF REALITY

Experiences come and go, but emotions linger with lasting psychological and physiological takeaways. Feelings and emotion are powerful things that constantly influence brain chemistry and neural circuitry patterns. These changes reflect attachments that filter and give context to future beliefs and experiences. The emotional narrative or story they write becomes children's reality and, ultimately, their destiny. The brain is built up through actual emotional experiences (Gerhardt, 2015). What goes in will ultimately determine what comes out. Shaping the minds of students is not a metaphorical mantra for teachers; it is a literal one.

Every emotional experience, fleeting or dramatic, joyous or painful, has lasting impacts on brain development, neural networks, and emotional attachments. In the context of education, this understanding is particularly important. Learning and social challenges at school are emotionally charged and account for a large proportion of attachments children will embrace as part of their developing personas.

Learning can be an exhilarating joyride for one and an emotional nightmare for the next. Even the most thoughtful, well-planned lesson is no guarantee of a rewarding learning experience. The battle lines are drawn. Will a child experience learning and life through the lens of joy, safety, and resilience, or will it be from a perspective of emotional pain and self-doubt?

EMOTIONAL ALIGNMENT, LEARNING, AND CONNECTION

Children come to school with their own unique set of experiences, beliefs, and neural network patterning that determines how an educational experience is processed.

Learning and social challenges at school are not a problem for emotionally balanced children hardwired to beliefs of bravery and resiliency. Exploration, risk, and challenge are exciting endeavors that come with abundant emotional reward. Curricular learning takes place, but a far greater outcome occurs as a direct result of the authentically rewarding experience. An emotionally rewarding learning experience supports normal brain development and neural circuitry that positively influences future learning and the capacity for a fulfilling connected life.

Things are not so easy for children disconnected from healthy beliefs and emotions. Life's journey has resulted in a different pattern of neurological wiring. These children tend to cope with the challenge of learning in unhealthy ways because experiences of the past have created that mold. Anxious physiological responses, fear, feelings of low self-worth, avoidance strategies, or outright dysfunctional behavior are the established way to navigate social and learning challenges. Regardless of their intelligence or capacity to learn, filtering experiences through unhealthy beliefs and emotions will always push students further from emotional balance and a healthy connection to learning.

> An old grandfather told his grandson, "My son, there's an old battle between two wolves inside us all. One is Evil. It is anger, jealousy, greed, resentment, inferiority, lies and ego. The other is Good. It is joy, peace, love, hope, humility, kindness, empathy and truth." Somewhat worried, the boy thought about it, then asked, "Grandfather, which wolf wins?" The old man replied, "The one you feed."
> —North American Legend

From a standpoint of healthy brain development, the obvious goal is to have children leave class each day feeling good about their educational experience. The challenge for teachers becomes all the emotional baggage and unhealthy stories children already possess and the sad realization that those most desperately in need of connection are often the ones to most fiercely deny it. If healthy connections feel so good, why is it so difficult for the disconnected to embrace them?

The simple answer is that disconnected experiences and emotional distress may be all they know. A more sinister perspective suggests the forces that distance children from healthy beliefs and lifestyles are sneaky and deceptive and may come with their own unconscious emotional rewards. Why else would a child embrace and hang on to unhealthy beliefs and engage in behavior that always ends in chronic drama and deepening emotional despair?

DISCONNECTION, NEURAL DYSREGULATION, AND EMOTIONAL ADDICTION

In an emotionally balanced person, the reward centers of the brain generate beta-endorphin payoffs that make us feel good in an effort to reinforce healthy choices and behaviors. Emotions like happiness, love, and self-worth are pleasurable and encourage connected behaviors that keep us centered. This effective reward system would lead us to believe that behavior always follows pleasurable feelings, but this is not always the case.

Attachment theorists beginning with Bowlby (1907–1990) have long suggested neglecting the basic human need for connection may lead to chemical and neural imbalance inhibiting normalized brain development (Bowlby, 1965). Children need connection as much as they ever have, but rising anxiety rates and disorders may suggest they are simply are not getting a large enough dose to nurture the attachments that help them feel safe, resilient, and worthy. The resulting neural dysregulation triggers a chronic survival mode state and a dependence on anxiety, anger, self-pity, and emotional dysfunction to cope with their distress.

Recent discoveries in neuroscience propose this type of neural dysregulation may result in unconscious biochemical addictions to stress hormones that act in remarkably similar ways to addictive drugs (Koob, 2008). These pain-killing hormones are free and readily available for those who know how to find them. All that is needed is a little, or a lot, of emotional drama. This may be an attractive option for disconnected children with no other alternative to cope with their enduring emotional distress. Teachers have always known that children get something out of chronic attention-seeking behaviors, bullying, procrastination, or "poor me" attitudes. Current neuroscience backs that up.

Teachers perceptive to the workings of emotional addiction can

- See dysfunctional behaviors for what they really are: **an unconscious drive for unhealthy emotional payoffs**

- Plan strategies to break the cycle of emotional and behavioral addictions

- Avoid emotional control dramas that feed all addiction

- See children as something greater than their dysfunction

EMOTIONAL ALIGNMENT AND HEALING

Fortunately, the human brain is resilient, and the same neural plasticity exposing it to dysregulation and out-of-balance states leaves room for the healing power of healthy experiences and authentic connections (Santa Barbara Graduate Institute Center for Clinical Studies and Research, n.d.). From a therapeutic and neurological perspective, it may be that teachers are positioned, better than anyone, to influence the physiology of a child's brain in healthy ways. They can control, manage, and monitor much of the emotional experience that can literally shape and heal the minds of children.

The Emotionally Connected Classroom is an innovative educational approach inspired by an addiction therapy model that teaches the disconnected how to weave authentic connections, behaviors, and thought patterns into their daily lives. Changing a life stuck in dysfunction and emotional pain takes more than talk. Curriculum-driven social and emotional learning objectives are meaningless fluff if not expressed as real experiences. It takes actual connected moments and authentic feelings to balance brain chemistry and prove a new narrative is possible. Emotions, joyful or uncomfortable, are the real tools of the teaching trade.

> *Connection is nature's multipurpose tool for nurturing emotional wellness and a healthy balanced brain. It can affect significant positive change in all aspects of a person's life. It is a simple but powerful solution for complex issues in an even more complicated world.*
>
> Todd Ritchey
> Emotional Addiction Specialist

> *Healthy emotional attachments are not taught, they are the product of actual connected emotional experiences.*

Emotions are not really good or bad as measured by levels of pleasure or discomfort. They all have purpose if embraced in proper context. In the world of education, feel-good emotions have the obvious upside, but uncomfortable feelings are also an expected and necessary component of learning, challenge, taking risks, and exploring the unknown. If anxious feelings or even physical pain are never experienced, children will never learn to manage, overcome, or value these challenges.

It may seem counterintuitive, but uncomfortable feelings, sometimes even painful ones, may be the most important and overlooked tool for emotional balance and healing. Overcoming anxious feelings is a thrilling, liberating, and joyful achievement. It takes fear to experience bravery and frustration to practice patience. The transition or journey from emotional discomfort to emotional balance is also the source of the most powerful healing.

This gets to the crux of the Emotionally Connected Classroom model. Empowering students to use thought patterns and emotions in healthy ways to learn, do big exciting things, share positive energy, and embrace life to the fullest is the greatest gift a teacher can give. Ultimately, it will be the experiences and emotions children choose to embrace that will dictate their destiny. It makes sense to begin every lesson with this in mind.

The Changing Role of Education

The education system that governs teaching and learning is a relic of the past century that has experienced only incremental changes in its attempt to meet the changing needs of children and society. The demands of an antiquated education structure dependent on curricular objectives, comparative testing, and control never seem to disappear, and they dominate a stressful learning experience. As a cultural whole, we have largely cast aside the natural drive to learn in a playful, adventurous, and cooperative way.

Simply put, learning has become stress-inducing work. This may represent the single greatest controllable disconnection in the lives of children. School is at least partially responsible for denying the free-spirited, connected experiences children need to develop in normal healthy ways. In many regards, the school experience has systematically nurtured anxious, disconnected children.

The skill sets for success in the twenty-first century have changed and revolve around healthy connections that nurture teamwork, intrapersonal skills, and free-flowing creative thought. Pressure for change exists, and new educational strategies have emerged to address whole child learning philosophies. Recently rewritten curriculum in British Columbia, Canada, demonstrates a trend toward a reduction in content and testing that leaves room for connected healthy learning experiences. Emotional wellness, communication, socioemotional skill sets, and connected student-centered learning experiences are at the center of the redesign of curriculum and assessment strategies (Government of British Columbia Ministry of Education, 2018). Emotionally balanced and resilient youth prepared for the challenges of a rapidly changing disconnected world is a new priority.

Curriculum will always matter, but at the end of the day, how a child feels about the learning experience is far more important than what they have learned. Fortunately, connected experiences and curriculum do not have to be an either-or proposition. We know emotionally unbalanced children chronically underperform and act out. We also know they are the time stealers in every class and consume much of a teacher's own emotional energy. The best student learning always relies on connected feelings and a playful adventurous spirit for inspired learning. Setting a daily connection intention helps teachers stay the course on the things they know matter most and creates a win-win scenario.

What has been missing for teachers is a practical approach that goes beyond talk and respects the challenges teachers and children face in existing educational systems. *The Emotionally Connected Classroom* offers a new definition of connectedness allowing teachers to develop their own socioemotional agenda best suited for the needs of each unique student or class. The Six Ps of Connection set the stage for healthy emotional reward and authentic attachments children need to emotionally thrive and learn. Together with an innovative lesson plan template, it becomes easy for teachers to drive out fear and integrate healthy connections into the everyday curricular learning experience.

Imagine If ...

The anxious, isolated, and painfully shy girl in your class who stumbles with debilitating fear when called on, the one who forces smiles to hide her pain and spends almost as much time away sick as she does in the classroom, leaves at the end of the day excited about school. At home, she greets her mother with an enthusiastic smile and shares the news of the day. Today she contributed in a group project, encouraged others, made a new friend, and most important, she felt good about it. Imagine the feeling of hope.

This is more than a dream. Stripping away the debilitating disconnecting forces of a modern culture, unhealthy attachments, and emotional addictions, reveals the authentic truth and potential that lies within every child. There is no need for excuses, labels, or drama to explain or justify behavior. There is only connection and authentic reward or disconnection and the unhealthy payoffs of emotional pain. An authentic choice may be difficult, but for students armed with healthy thinking patterns and authentic support, it becomes a viable attractive option in spite of the powerful disconnecting forces that surround us all. It is a sad commentary on the education system when students graduate not knowing how to feel good or be their best. It is time to teach them. It is time to feed their "Good Wolf."

The journey begins with a bold proclamation for transformational change and a willingness to forge a new path, a paradigm shift that allows teachers and students to view the world and the learning experience in a new light. The journey begins with a trip back in time to rediscover the biological truth of who we are as humans. Our children are hunter-gatherers who need each other. Connection is not a luxury, it is a matter of survival.

Getting the Most out *The Emotionally Connected Classroom*

- **Think mindset**. *The Emotionally Connected Classroom* is a mindset, framework, or lens for viewing learning process rather than a package of lessons or strategies for all grades or subject areas. Examples of strategies, lessons, case studies, and vignettes attempt to bring theory to life, but the best strategy for understanding remains with shifting perspectives. Thinking like a Hunter-Gatherer in Chapter 1 is a good start.

- **Consider your best lessons.** Value, filter, and fine-tune what you already do well through a new lens. Best lessons are always student-centered connected experiences. Be the expert in connection you already are.

- **Experiences shape who you are.** Experiences and emotions in the classroom always influence neural connections, emotional attachments, and brain capacity. The book attempts to keep the brain science accessible and usable. Be a budding neuroscientist. Teach your students to be one, too!

- **Reflect on past practice.** Take time to analyze past practice, learning experiences, and student interactions. Could a new way of thinking have changed things?

- **Personal introspection**. Feel free to drift and reflect on your own life connections and experiences. Real change starts with a teacher's personal relationship with connectedness.

- **Take a first step**. It can be a strategy, a lesson, or a unit. It takes an actual experience to create belief. Connection perfection is not necessary, and it always takes time. The only step that matters is the first one.

- **Recruit others.** Community is a cornerstone of connectedness. Sharing an action plan with other teachers will clarify thoughts, foster collaboration, and help make a new direction feel less intimidating.

- **Embrace your emotions as you read.** This book is all about the emotional experience.

CHAPTER 1

Hunter-Gatherers, Survival, and the Classroom

The human world has never experienced constant change and motion in the way that it does today. Cultural beliefs, lifestyles, and the foods we eat are as fleeting as the latest great advertising campaign or fashion trend. Advances in science and the wonders of the digital age add to the belief that we have evolved beyond hunter-gatherer physiology.

THINK ABOUT IT

Hunter-gatherer physiology had 2.5 million years to evolve during the Paleolithic period. Only 330 generations have passed since the development of agriculture. Modern-day cultural shifts are measured in decades or less. That is a mere drop in the bucket in the eyes of evolutionary processes.

Evolution has not been able to keep pace, not even remotely so. Disconnection is an understandable side effect of this juxtaposition, and children experience this change fastest of all. The fact that they have the least control over these changes adds to their rising anxiety. They are ill prepared for the challenges this disconnection poses to their learning, health, and emotional wellness. Their hunter-gatherer physiology is in a fight for survival, and it is nothing less than a traumatic experience.

Children are struggling, and they need help bridging the gap. Human physiology will not change any time soon and the likelihood that unhealthy modern-day pressures will suddenly retreat is equally improbable. School environments are somewhat controllable, and individual classrooms are even more so. School may be the only opportunity for a child to embrace the natural truthful version of their biology.

HUNTER-GATHERERS AND THE EVOLUTION OF CONNECTEDNESS

The environmental context of hunter-gatherer life is largely responsible for shaping the human brain and human behavior (Wright, 1994). Survival was a challenge in the world of the hunter-gatherer. In response, tribal communities evolved to mitigate potential threats through communal, stable, safe environments (Lee, 1988). Working together and sharing provided the regular food source needed to reduce the very real possibility of starvation. The physical safety and security of tribal connections allowed the hunter-gatherer to focus efficiently on their daily business, increasing their potential for meaningful contributions to the greater good. Cultures evolved to nurture, value, and celebrate beliefs aligned with tribal bonds and contributions. Working hard for the collective whole was important—as long as there was still ample time to share their stories and laugh around the campfire.

Survival was not the only reason they stayed together. Pleasurable emotions paralleled their dependence on tribal connections. Feelings of safety, love, and self-value were not coincidental occurrences. They were a product of natural selection and a physiological response to the need for connection. The link between connected beliefs, behaviors, and biochemical rewards strengthened. This important evolutionary adaptation supported tribal connections and allowed humans to experience love, belonging, purpose, and the joy of supporting others in very real ways.

Connection was important and played a role in every aspect of hunter-gatherer society. Opportunities to share with their loved ones and contribute to the greater good were never difficult to find.

SURVIVAL MODE

On a daily basis, the collective energies of the tribe provided a safe environment, but warfare, predatory attack, illness, and injuries remained significant threats. Sometimes these types of exceptional circumstances required an elevated state of alertness where the hunter-gatherer needed to think fast, react quickly, or deal with the pain of potential trauma. Desperate times initiated survival mode.

The release of stress hormones helped prepare the hunter-gatherer for the challenge ahead. Dopamine increased alertness and the desire to act quickly, cortisol optimized the most necessary bodily functions at the expense of others, and endorphins eased pain in the case of injury (Montgomery & Ritchey, 2008). Typically, the elevated state of alertness assumed one of three forms.

1. **Fight response:** Fight the lion.

2. **Flight response:** Run from the lion.

3. **Freeze response:** Hide from the lion.

Each survival response offered a strategy designed to optimize the ability to escape the survival threat. An incorrect choice or a casual response could result in a poor fight or a short race, but in general, the adaptation was quite effective in helping hunter-gatherers avoid or deal with temporary threats.

Survival mode was a purposeful survival adaptation, but extended exposure was stressful on the body resulting in uncomfortable states of chronic pain, illness, anxiety, and depression. Certainly, this would not be beneficial for the day-to-day life of the hunter-gatherer. Under normal conditions, hunter-gatherer physiology would rebalance once danger receded. The lion shows up and triggers a survival response. Fight hard, run fast, or hide really well, and survival is achieved. The problem is solved, and survival mode is no longer necessary. Hormone levels rebalance, and life goes on as normal.

How did the hunter-gatherer transition from terrified or intensely enraged to relaxed and balanced? One would tend to fixate on an experience marked by the warm breath and the jagged teeth of a lion, but the hunter-gatherer could always count on some help to bring stress hormone levels back to normal.

THE HOMEOSTATIC DRIVE: A TEAM EFFORT

The homeostatic drive is an evolutionary adaptation designed to keep all living creatures within acceptable norms for optimal healthy conditions (Montgomery & Ritchey, 2010). When the human body is knocked out of ideal parameters, it attempts to self-regulate and rebalance. If we are too hot or cold, our physiology responds with sweating or shivering. There is no need for us to think about it or do anything. Things change considerably if we are so cold that our body cannot manage the circumstance. Conscious thought tells us to put on a jacket, sit by the campfire, or share a warm hug. A potentially life-threatening scenario is averted.

When we are emotionally out of balance, our body also tries to bring us back to relaxed norms. This can be a challenge if the trauma is particularly intense or conditions are such that the anxiety-inducing trigger does not go away. The most reasonable course of action would be to remove one's self from the imminent threat or stressor and embrace close connections with loved ones that inspire feelings of safety.

The hunter-gatherer was in all probability completely unaware of the physiological reflexes the homeostatic drive provided, but the powerful influence of tribal connections was a conscious factor in their efforts to rebalance in stressful times. In the life of an otherwise healthy connected hunter-gatherer, the anxious survival mode experience was less than pleasurable, and the desire to return to the more pleasant feelings of safety, support, and love of the tribe was significant. Strong connections with these healthy emotions were an attractive alternative that encouraged the hunter-gatherer to let go of the intense anger or fear associated with their survival experience. It remains true today that an important component of regulating painful emotions is cultivating positive ones (Barker, n.d.).

Hunter-gatherer children came into the world biologically bound to embrace love, support, bravery, and a willingness to contribute, but connections and the skill sets to make them effective still had to be nurtured. From birth through childhood, and into their adult lives, they learned and practiced connection skills, thought patterns, and behaviors as part of their daily lives. Connections and contributions, both large and small, were a big deal.

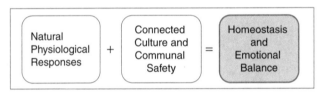

Natural physiological responses work in harmony with authentic connections to help humans rebalance in times of stress.

TRIBAL CONNECTIONS, SURVIVAL, AND LOW STATUS

Reliable food sources, love, and belonging were very important aspects of a hunter-gatherer's life because they enhanced safety in both physical and emotional ways. If disconnected from the tribe, fearful anticipation of starvation or predatory animals and almost certain death became a significant threat. The loss of highly valued emotional connections was equally traumatic. Disconnection from the tribe was such a serious matter that simply the thought of separation could trigger a very real biochemical survival response.

Hierarchy and status were not usually significant components of day-to-day tribal life (Montgomery & Ritchey, 2010). There was no real personal wealth or accumulation of goods to say that one member was above the other. The tribe benefitted when all members felt safe and supported because this enabled them to contribute to the best of their ability. Self-worth helped them feel good about their prospects as a valued member and added to feelings of security. However, in truly difficult times when tribal survival itself was at risk, that belief could be tested.

In challenging times, survival of the tribe trumped individual needs, and the expulsion of members who contributed less or proved a liability was a possibility. Hunter-gatherers feeling less certain about their value or connection with the tribe would be highly motivated to try a little harder to prove themselves an asset. If they were unable to do so, anxious feelings limited the ability to function and contribute effectively, further exacerbating their plight.

Under these conditions, feelings of "less than" and the survival state that they would likely trigger could be unrelenting even if separation was not imminent or more bountiful times returned. Few things were more frightening than disconnection from those they loved or the safety of the tribe. Hunter-gatherers were fortunate this was an unusual scenario in their cooperative supportive culture.

THINK ABOUT IT

Status in school is an entrenched driver of the educational experience. Low status for many is the outcome. This is a stressful anomaly for our hunter-gatherer brains. Status-driven stressors at school:

- Competitive tests
- Assessment by grades
- Social hierarchies
- Separation by grade levels
- Separation by learning or behavioral capacities
- Principal, teacher, and student hierarchies

EVOLUTIONARY MISMATCH

The cultural and social environment in which we live today is an anomaly or mismatch with our biological evolution (Lieberman, 2013). Our society has come a long way from the life of a hunter-gatherer. Gone are the threats of wild animals, starvation, and tribal warfare. Yet it remains true, biologically speaking, that our brains and bodies remain those of a hunter-gatherer.

One key variance is that we experience stress in a very different way. Modern-day stress is a consequence of social conditions—our jobs, unhealthy relationships, and unrealistic cultural expectations. For students, it may be the result of challenges with grades, peer status, belonging, bullying, or isolation.

Today we are rarely, if ever, in jeopardy of starvation or predatory death, yet survival mode traits such as anxiety, fear, and anger are growing concerns. The disconnecting effects of cultural pressures and isolation feel the same and are just as physiologically and psychologically real as that experienced by a hunter-gatherer threatened by a lion or separated from his community. The differentiator is that modern stressors and social conditions do not go away. Problems at work or school will probably exist tomorrow and beyond. This poses a troubling scenario for modern humans because the strong authentic connections and balanced environments needed to aid in the return to a healthier homeostatic state do not typically exist in the way they once did for our ancestors. The disconnected are trapped in survival states marked by emotional stress and pain. The resulting health and wellness issues are significant, and children may be paying the greatest price of all.

There is a significant rift between how we live and how our bodies are designed to function. Hunter-gatherer physiology evolved to suit the culture and environment in which they lived, but it is poorly adapted to modern cultural settings and lifestyles.

CHRONIC ANXIETY AND MENTAL ILLNESS: THE SILENT TRAGEDY

"Kids just aren't as tough as they used to be."
Baby-Boomer Proverb

It is an interesting point to ponder, and more interesting yet that dismissive blame given to the children themselves is often the response. A slow-moving tragedy is unfolding before our eyes, and it involves our most precious resource. A sharp accelerating increase in mental health issues for children is reaching epidemic proportions. Regardless of where we place responsibility, it is becoming increasingly difficult to dismiss a very real problem.

- An estimated 31.9% of adolescents have had an anxiety disorder (National Institute of Mental Health, 2005)

- 42% increase in parent-reported ADHD (Visser et al., 2014)

- The 12-month prevalence of a major depressive episode for adolescents increased 30% between 2005 and 2014 (Mojtabai, Olfson, & Han, 2016)

- 100% increase in ten- to fourteen-year-old suicide rates from 1999–2014 (Centers for Disease Control and Prevention, 2016)

Survival Mode in the Classroom

Health, emotional wellness, authentic cultural connections, and the ability to learn are codependent. The natural inclination for educators is to prioritize learning, but any missing link adversely affects the others. Teaching and learning is their job, but efforts may go unrewarded if broader issues remain unattended. There may be some reluctance on the part of schools to accept responsibility, but the point is moot. A one-dimensional approach is wasted energy that inevitably leads to an escalation in the survival response. Expecting students with emotional or health issues to embrace competitive learning challenges on an uneven playing field is both unfair and unjust.

Dysfunctional behavior is often a reflection of a survival mode response. A child traumatized by abuse may fearfully shut down or lash out as a bully. Likewise, a dangerous medical condition, accident, or loss of a loved one is a justifiable trigger for any survival response, but the underlying driver of most dysfunction is usually far more discreet. People may not consider disconnection when they think of traumatic emotional experiences, but our biology always does.

The behaviors and beliefs students attach to as they struggle to cope with the unhealthy feelings of disconnection can vary widely. Some are subtle, while others can affect the entire class culture and consume much of a teacher's time and energy. Attempts to control or manage behaviors may have little long-term effect if the underlying cause of the student's dysfunction remains. Acting out in unhealthy ways will exist as their most viable coping strategy as long as disconnection and emotional pain persists.

What Does Survival Mode in the Classroom Look Like?

Intense emotion, panic, or destructive uncontrollable behavior comes to the forefront of many people's thoughts when they think of survival mode. They are not wrong, but they are if they limit survival mode to these parameters. The vast majority of cases will not look like that at all, and dismissing responses that do not appear as pressing or dangerous may be a serious mistake. All coping strategies driven by unhealthy emotional attachments are dangerous because they have the potential and tendency to escalate into something far more dangerous. The challenge for teachers is recognizing the subtler expressions of survival mode before they become overwhelming and chronic.

The coping strategy a student in survival mode may connect with or attach to will vary. A fight response in the classroom is hardly difficult to spot. Flight is disruptive but perceived as less dangerous. These types of avoidance strategies are common and generally identifiable as unhealthy coping responses. The most difficult expression of survival mode to identify is the freeze response. It is discreet and by far the most prevalent.

- **Fight:** The aggressive suppression of the fight response at school occurs because it has the perception of being most dangerous.

- **Flight:** Avoidance of activities is marginally accepted as a better option. Sometimes flight is literal because students skip school. Others bounce nervously in their chair as their flight response is vigorously controlled by classroom rules.

- **Freeze:** Hidden, unseen, and less disruptive, this survival mode response can easily be overlooked.

Freeze is the most common response because it is the most acceptable way of coping in a school setting and may be the student's only viable option to express her distress. In traditional school environments, it may even be considered a positive behavior worthy of celebration. It is easy to understand how a teacher could miss the discreet nature of the freeze response in the face of the more troublesome behaviors of fight or flight. This makes it far more dangerous because the distressed student is more likely to go without help.

If teachers are cognizant of trauma that a student has experienced, then it certainly merits a watchful eye, but it is more likely than not that a student's emotional history and experiences that drive survival mode behaviors will be unavailable to them. Students come to school with secrets, and parents may or may not inform teachers of hot spots to watch for. Counselor reports are more likely to include diagnosed labels than emotional trauma or neglect a student has experienced. While knowing emotional history may be advantageous, it is not completely necessary. The more important factor is a teacher's conscious intent to look for chronic unhealthy emotions and recognize survival mode behaviors.

Fortunately, the survival response and unhealthy coping strategies are easy to spot. The sad part is that a willful glance at an average classroom will also reveal how widespread the problem is.

The Many Faces of Survival Mode and Classroom Anxiety

- A "good" student always does his work but rarely interacts with others.

- An ADHD problem student bounces in his seat with no avenue to expel his nervous energy. His face is flushed, and his body twitches.

- A girl freezes during a speech; she looks pale and stiff.

- A student knows the material yet always bombs on the tests.

- A student with a disability or special needs feels uncomfortably different.

- A top performer is under pressure to excel and studies excessively. He wears an artificial smile to hide his pain.

- The weirdo suffers from mood swings (angry-sad-fearful).

- A depressed kid avoids healthy fun activities.

- Another tries hard, but she has an extremely difficult time learning and concentrating. She complains that her brain feels foggy.

- A poor performer embraces the class clown persona for peer approval.

- The victim is afraid of just about everything. The bully knows it and lurks nearby.

NOTE. Survival mode responses are never a reflection of a student's truth. Unfortunately, the coping mechanism he embraces can easily lead to unjustified and painful labels that unfairly define him.

DISCONNECTION FROM NATURAL LEARNING AND EDUCATIONAL INSTINCTS

The hunter-gatherers had much to learn, and they had to learn it well. Their survival depended on it. Over time, the transmission of cultural knowledge became more important. The detailed knowledge and skills related to hunting, gathering, processing foods, protection strategies, and health care went far beyond what any one individual or small group could discover on their own (Gray, 2013). Effective socialization, communication and connections with others became very important to the transmission of knowledge. A dependence on education evolved, but it looked much different from the schooling students experience today.

Philosopher and naturalist Karl Groos (1898) argued that natural selection led to a strong drive in human children to observe the activities of elder tribe members and incorporate what they saw into play. Human beings are naturally curious and are intrinsically motivated to explore and experience the world around them. Hunter-gatherer culture took advantage of the natural drive to learn through play, exploration, and self-education. Children had few responsibilities and were free to observe, mimic, play, cooperate, socialize, and embrace adventure (Gray, 2013). Sharing new discoveries with their friends was an important means for acquiring knowledge and developing creative ideas.

Educational researcher Dr. Sugata Mitra's (2003) "Hole in the wall" experiments have shown that in the absence of supervision or formal teaching, students can teach themselves and each other. In 1999, his team of researchers dug a hole in a wall bordering an urban slum in New Delhi, installed an Internet-connected PC, and left it there. With no adult interference, hundreds of underprivileged students became computer literate within a few months. Mitra surmised that the students' natural curiosity, playfulness, sociability, self-organization, and willingness to experiment were the key factors in the learning successes.

In many regards, modern schooling exists in stark contrast to natural biological drives and the cultural traditions of hunter-gatherer learning. It is predominantly a top-down approach where adults dictate what students learn and how they learn it. The healthy emotional payoffs inspiring the instinct and will to learn have been set aside for a pressure-filled experience of testing, competition, and deadlines.

Hunter-Gatherers in the Classroom

The hunter-gatherer classroom theme is valuable because it illustrates the biological importance of connectedness. It also provides a beginning or reference point for students trying to discover their authentic self and embrace the things they know will bring them joy. This biological commonality sets the stage for a practical and manageable approach allowing teachers to address the authentic emotional needs of unique individuals in the classroom; one that transcends race, gender, culture, and socioeconomic realities. Regardless of what they may outwardly express, all students come genetically wired to care about others, contribute to the greater good, and learn. This was the case for their ancestors and remains the foundation of the true self for every modern student.

Thinking like a hunter-gatherer doesn't mean we have to be one or live like one. It is just an excellent way to remind us of authentic beliefs and behaviors that exist in harmony with our biology. The hunter-gatherers had an advantage in this regard because their culture nurtured connectedness and they experienced very real survival pressures that reminded them to stay connected. We do not share the same culture or experience the same pressures that made connection so important.

A conscious and diligent effort to know who we are and what really matters to us is more important than ever. This is especially true for students struggling to navigate their way through unhealthy cultural messages and an education system not aligned with their authentic needs.

Our common ancestry may provide the grounding for authentic connection, but a cookie-cutter definition of "connectedness" fitting all students and classes falls short. Each student and class is unique and is always changing. A new socioemotional curricular agenda must be equally dynamic and designed in a way to help students discover their own sense of self. A life aligned with the essence of a student's true self maximizes the potential for emotional balance, health, and learning. In the next chapter, we look beyond the hunter-gatherer definition of connectedness and discover what it might look like in modern schools.

Inubu

From Survival to Safety: Homeostasis

Inubu was terrified, but he felt more alive than ever. Subtle sounds of the quiet forest echoed crisply in his ears. The leaves on the bush seemed to come alive as his vision intensified. In a violent rush, the bush burst open. Uncontrollably, he began to cry.

Jabari, his mother's brother, had come to save him. His knees buckled with an overwhelming release of emotions. He would not die this day, but the realization of his situation turned his thoughts to the oncoming onslaught of Jabari's anger. This man had hunted dangerous beasts and fearlessly fought off invading tribes. Inubu's carelessness had ruined the hunt, and his fear once again began to rise. The smile on his uncle's face told another truth. Too weak to stand on his own, he was lifted by the hunter's powerful arms. No words were spoken as he carried Inubu back to the village in the early morning light.

Inubu wasn't sure if he slept on the journey. Fatigue had overwhelmed him, but a feeling of peace and safety flowed through his body as they approached his settlement. A tear of happiness rolled down his cheek as thoughts turned to his mother. He knew she would be worried. Jabari set him on his feet.

"This lesson has been a difficult one. Wipe your tears and walk into the village a proud hunter warrior."

Moments before, Inubu felt like he had failed. But the truth was that he had survived the night alone and indeed he would be more careful next time. Maybe his mistake made him stronger.

Together they walked into the village to joyful hoots and hollers. Later that evening as they gathered around the fire, Inubu's experience was shared as animated stories of bravery. His mother smiled at him as his younger brother suckled on her breast. It did not seem long ago that his own comfort was found there. Reconnected with the tribe, he finally felt like he could breathe once again. He would recover from this day. His proud father sat beside his uncle. One day, Inubu would be a great protector, too.

CHAPTER 2

Connection Intentions, the Good Wolf, and the Six Ps

Curricular demands and grade standards for university entrance have driven our school structure for a very long time. Subjective reports comparing schools and classrooms add pressure to stick to traditional teaching approaches. Nonetheless, there is a general consensus among teachers, researchers, and governing educational bodies that connected students are happier and are less likely to engage in unhealthy behaviors. Even grade- and curriculum-focused traditionalists find it difficult to deny the empirical evidence that suggests academic achievement significantly improves with healthy connections (Blum & Libby, 2004). There is a growing movement in education to make connection a greater priority, but taking action remains difficult because opinions defining the scope of connection vary significantly. This chapter defines a whole-student connection perspective and uses the Six Ps (People, Purpose, Play, Passions, Present Thinking, and Personal Challenge) to set identifiable targets for connected learning experiences.

CONNECTION: A PHYSIOLOGICAL AND PHILOSOPHICAL DEFINITION

From a physiological perspective, *authentic connection* is any belief, behavior, or feeling with the potential to trigger a healthy, emotional payoff. Connectedness may not carry the same importance in matters of survival that it once did, but it remains important to our physiology. Authentic connections are the natural way to support health, biological norms, and emotional balance. Spending time with those we love, engaging in purposeful activities, play, pursuing passions, living in the moment, and delving into the unknown world of exploration and learning challenge, all potentiate, feel-good, endorphin payoffs. Authentic connections are important because they

- Trigger a physiological response allowing humans to experience authentic joy, self-worth, and fulfilment

- Nurture a sense of safety and help our physiology rebalance in times of difficulty

- Play an important role in healthy attachment acquisition

From a philosophical perspective, *authentic connection* refers to all experiences, beliefs, or emotions that push us toward our own personal definition of authentic truth. Identifying authentic truths provides tangible targets for healthy emotional reward and spiritual alignment. Without connection targets, we may become lost and forget the things that matter most. Inevitably, less authentic modern-day extrinsic pressures or emotional trauma will knock us off track. Connection is our pathway back to our own personal truth and emotional balance. It is our safe place.

> *"The ultimate goal of emotional and psychological healing is the dissolution of the false self and the discovery of the true self."*
> —Philosopher Carl Jung (1966)

Finally, *connectedness* is the measure to which one aligns her daily life with authentic behaviors, beliefs, and feelings. A person may maintain a set of authentic beliefs but consciously or unconsciously live life in a different way. This is the definition of disconnection. Connectedness is not a part-time affair. It matters all the time, and it is advantageous for teachers and students alike to know who they are, where they are, and where they should be headed. "Teaching students, not curriculum" is a common mantra of great teachers. This is authentic connection thinking. At the end of the day, connected experiences are what fill the hearts, souls, and minds of students in a lasting way.

The old man shared a valuable lesson with his grandson. Connected healthy emotional experience is how we feed our Good Wolf. Curriculum is only the backdrop in a meaningful learning experience. How will your lesson design and daily connection intention feed the Good Wolf and starve the Evil One?

IMAGE SOURCE: iStock.com/andyworks

CONNECTION IN THE CLASSROOM

Educational experiences can be interesting or boring, fulfilling or seemingly senseless, joyful or emotionally painful. Connectedness and the healthy emotional payoffs it provides are the lynch pin. Embracing authentic feelings as a primary target in lesson design sets the Emotionally Connected Classroom apart because it addresses a chronic shortcoming in the modern classroom. Many students do not know where to find authentic payoffs or how to "feel" authentic reward in big ways.

An effective connection objective will always target an experience with the expectation that a healthy physiological response, feeling, or belief will follow. This outcome signifies the potential formation of authentic emotional attachments and is an excellent indicator of meaningful lasting learning. "Today my learning experience felt amazing, and I want to do that again."

Setting Connection Intentions

Every traditional lesson plan begins with prescribed learning objectives that drive the remainder of the lesson. Learning to spell, calculate, make, do, or recite something becomes the final product. In the Emotionally Connected Classroom lesson template (Chapter 9), the traditional curricular objective remains, but a connectedness objective always accompanies it. Yes, math and bravery can and should mix!

The connection objective is responsible for driving the learning process, reflection, and assessment. A connected authentically rewarding learning experience becomes the target or product for students. Content outcomes remain valued entities on their own, but they are not the ultimate benchmark for whether meaningful learning has taken place. The emotion or belief attachment is far more powerful, longer lasting, and more influential than curricular outcomes for future learning. This makes it a more important measure of authentic learning than any test or curricular product.

The concept is simple. Factoring equations with a friend is more fun. Peer coaching breed's ownership and purpose and elevates the desire to set high standards as a team. A partner setting high standards for measurements in a science lab has a purposeful rewarding task to guide him. Learning to communicate in positive ways makes any activity more pleasurable. A connection with bravery, purpose, or competence will always reduce fear and improve performance. Overcoming self-doubt is liberating and always gratifying. "I can't believe I did it!"

When it comes to traditional curricular learning outcomes, some are more likely than others to trigger a pleasurable emotional response, but this does not necessarily mean the curricular objective is destined to be less enjoyable. Wrapping or packaging a less stimulating lesson with something that feels authentically rewarding changes the experience. A connection-based curriculum does not compete with traditional curriculum outcomes. It supercharges them!

A bold proclamation supporting a connection objective as a lesson priority is a tangible demonstration of a paradigm shift. Elevating the status of

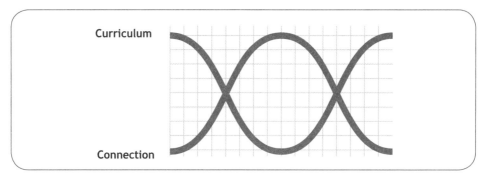

Curriculum

Connection

Curricular learning offers a limitless backdrop for connected experiences. Connection inspires joyful rewarding learning! They work best together.

connection in the learning process begins with a compelling sales pitch to create a sense of believable priority. This is important because students are used to product-based learning that ends with testing and comparative results. Consistent integration of connection intentions and assessment into daily lessons nurtures a reliable expectation that normalizes it as part of the learning process.

Teachers use strategies like Think-Pair-Share to create opportunity for healthy interactions, but there is no guarantee students will buy in on the socioemotional objective. Their attention can easily drift to the curricular task alone. Setting a daily connection intention acts as a promise or binding commitment to feed the Good Wolf. It is a first step students can take to own and self-assess their experience. Embracing a connection intention comes with an enticing promise of feel-good rewards, but the benefits for students may be far more consequential than a pleasurable experience alone.

What if feeding the Good Wolf actually affected brain physiology in a way that made students happier, more resilient, and smarter than ever thought possible? Growing evidence strongly suggests healthy thinking patterns and effort can, in fact, make students smarter and happier. In her book, *Mindset*, Carol Dweck (2006) suggests IQ and socioemotional traits are not a fixed condition. For students accepting this belief as true, the attraction of connection intentions becomes a target worth owning. Her research also suggests a growth mindset is what allows students to love what they are doing and helps them persevere and overcome. Fixed and growth mindset theory aligns nicely with process/product learning, connection/disconnection themes, and of course, grandfather's Good Wolf/Bad Wolf story.

Nonetheless, this is a difficult story for students to grasp when they believe judgment, failure, fear, and anxiety are their fixed destiny. Teachers can quote research and tell an inspirational, vivid story, but what students need is real, focus-connected experiences to prove it is both possible and true. Daily connection intentions are the first chapter in writing a new believable story.

A Daily Connection Intention is how students will feed the Good Wolf and infuse healthy thoughts and emotional payoffs into learning experiences.

IMAGE SOURCE: Pixabay.com/steffiheufelder

Example:

> **Today I will:**
>
> - Be brave
> - Be supportive, be a cheerleader
> - Contribute
>
> - Value myself, value others
> - Be resilient, make big mistakes
> - Say no to anxiety and the Bad Wolf

Frances Friend Fourth-Grade Math

Walton Elementary Case Study

Fran liked to use games and puzzles to teach challenging math concepts. She also valued the activity as a great opportunity to nurture social skills, create community, foster creativity, and make learning fun. These types of intentions were important to her, but she wondered how important they were to her students. When students played the games, did they even know these connections were supposed to be the most important part of the experience? Play the game and hopefully these intangible objectives will happen wasn't good enough for her. The approach felt passive and random.

> *There is a big difference between playing a game to learn something and playing a game to nurture an authentic learning experience and lasting attachment.*

Teachers are on the right track when they embrace connection intentions to foster healthy attachments. However, unless students embrace an intention as their own, the emotional attachment the teacher is hoping for lacks focus and outcomes may be random or weak. The transference of ownership from teacher strategy to student ownership becomes the challenge and priority. A secondary problem for students is that all these objectives are incredibly complex and require specific skill sets or emotional attachments they may lack. In the world of targeted attachment building, less is usually more. Mrs. Friend simplified her objectives and used different intentions with specific achievable and assessable targets for similar games over several lessons.

> **Curricular Intention:** Play a game to practice addition and/or subtraction skills.
>
> **Connection Intention:** Culture building—Create a sense of belonging and equality. Task—Play with a new partner or multiple partners. Smile, practice warm welcomes, and share good energy. Help make a new friend feel good and part of the team.

> **Curricular Intention:** Play a game to practice addition and/or subtraction skills.
>
> **Connection Intention:** Help or graciously be helped. Contribute. It feels good to help someone. Graciously accept help. Listen, try hard, and say thank you.

> **Curricular Intention:** Play a game to practice addition and/or subtraction skills.
>
> **Connection Intention:** Set communal targets, cooperate, and celebrate big. Winning together feels amazing. Practice the skills of unbridled celebration.

> **Curricular Intention:** Play a game to practice addition and/or subtraction skills.
>
> **Connection Intention:** Healthy competition. Try hard and value effort over win–lose perspectives. Your best always feels good, and sometimes magic happens. Practice sportsmanship and humble victory and joyfully embrace the successes of others (people like that a lot). Looking good when you lose means you always win.

NOTE. Mrs. Friend loves a noisy active classroom, and intentions make it happen in a purposeful way.

I GET IT! BUT WHERE DOES A TEACHER FIND THESE INTENTIONS?

Children are not hunter-gatherers struggling to survive, but they share common biological truths governing healthy beliefs and emotional payoffs. A framework to define authentic belief and behaviors helps create targets for daily connection intentions linking learning and healthy emotional reward.

THE SIX Ps OF CONNECTION: FOOD FOR THE GOOD WOLF

Experiences in a disconnected culture cloud student's beliefs regarding who they are and what brings them joy. Through no fault of their own, many have been unconsciously feeding the wrong wolf for far too long. If an activity is not fun or rewarding on some level, the natural inclination is to quit and move on to something else. The Six Ps are a simple way to help teachers and students organize and clarify their thoughts about their authentic core values and the emotional payoffs they pursue. They are the motivator of any rewarding learning experience and a key component in the development of healthy emotional attachments (see Figure 2.1).

FIGURE 2.1

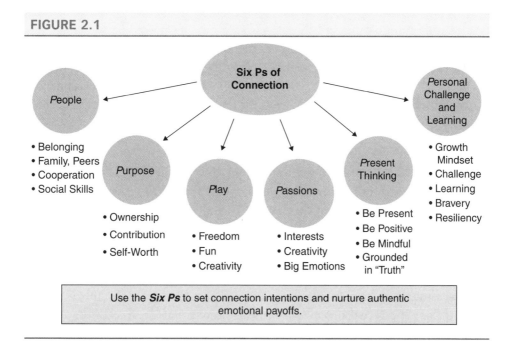

Use the **Six Ps** to set connection intentions and nurture authentic emotional payoffs.

CONNECTIONS WITH PEOPLE

Healthy connections with people provide feelings of safety and belonging. Meeting this basic human need nurtures a more relaxed, creative, and productive state. In the context of education, this type of connection is particularly important because learning demands taking risks and experiencing uncomfortable moments that threaten feelings of safety.

"No learning can take place without a significant relationship."
—James Comey, Professor of Child Psychiatry at the Yale Child Study Center

Young children are wholly dependent on their parents for feelings of love and safety. When children move on to school, teachers make a concerted effort to nurture respectful relationships and environments for students needing to belong and feel safe. As children mature, peer influence becomes more important as they attempt to discover their identity and pursue passions with a sense of independence. Peer connections at school play an important role in the development of belief systems. These relationships serve as a new kind of support independent from parents and teachers that ease the transition from childhood to maturity. The potential for influence is significant, and in the lives of teens, it may be the most powerful and rewarding connection of all. Teachers understand that peer connections matter a great deal and harvesting the energy they possess can prove to be an invaluable asset in the learning process.

School-wide culture can also be a safe haven for students needing to belong, feel safe, and identify with something beyond their own personal identity. School clubs, teams, and daily classroom experiences offer opportunities to build meaningful connections that may otherwise be missing in the lives of students. The vast majority of peer relationships begin at school, and for the fortunate, lifetime friendships will endure.

Any achievement feels better when celebrated with those we love, and the emotional pain of failure drifts away with a friendly hug or kind word. Parents, teachers, counselors, and even peers know that their capacity to influence is directly proportional to the strength of connections with others. If the relationship shares common beliefs and has a foundation of trust, students will follow. In an authentic connected relationship, there is a good feeling about guiding or being guided toward healthy authentic behaviors and rewards.

The vast amount of knowledge we need to navigate the world is well beyond the means of any individual dependent on self-discovery alone. Sociability is what allows knowledge to spread easily and quickly. We learn more and enjoy learning more when we do it with others.

Sample Connection Intentions for PEOPLE

- **Share healthy energy.** Smiles, laughter, and fun are contagious. Be fun. Model, teach, and practice the skills of fun.

- **Be social.** Nurture new connections. Partner up with someone new.

- **Think communal safety.** Make a formal intent or pledge for collective safety.

- **Value cultural identities.** Cultural identity is an important part of truth. Value differences and share them. Tell stories, read books, eat new food, and sing anthems or cultural songs. Engage in learning projects that elevate the value of different cultures. Different is exciting and interesting. Content and ideas are limitless. Celebrate differences.

- **Communal success.** Think team, communal goals. Great leaders elevate the game of the team. Value the assist; it is still a goal if someone else scores it.

NOTE. More intentions with People in supplementary materials (pages 173-175).

CONNECTIONS WITH PURPOSE

Psychologist David Yeager and his colleagues (2012) were not surprised when their research revealed that many students believed making money, attaining fame, and job satisfaction were important when asked about their hopes, dreams, and life goals. However, many also spoke of wanting to make a positive impact on their community or society by becoming a doctor who cares for people, or a pastor who "makes a difference." The interesting caveat the researchers found was that the teens with these "pro-social" types of goals tended to rate their schoolwork as more personally meaningful (Yeager, Bundick, & Johnson, 2012).

Purpose is about contribution, self-worth, and the legacy one leaves behind. A person contributing to the greater good is an asset and increases her status as a valued member of the group. Opportunities to contribute in the classroom can nurture a believable story of self-worth and can be a powerful motivator for personal growth. Maximizing our capacity to contribute requires one to be at his best. A best effort means growing, hard work, bravery, teamwork, and perseverance. In the context of learning, these are very valuable objectives.

Purpose is grounded in responsibility and ownership. It is human nature to find things forced on us less rewarding. At school, students struggle with being constantly told what to do and how to do it. A student-centered classroom is an ideal environment to learn about purpose because the opportunity to contribute is almost limitless. Students care deeply about their classmates and want to make a difference in their lives. The mantra for purpose in a Connected Classroom is simple: "How can I contribute and make my class better?" Positive influence in the lives of others feels amazing.

Sample Connection Intentions for PURPOSE

- **Seek out classmates in need.** Be intuitive, read the energy of others, especially those you do not know well

- **Value yourself.** You are only great if you share it. Trust that you have something to contribute. Be brave and share what you know or can do.

- **Value others.** Practice supportive language. Compliments feel good. A kind and thoughtful critique feels great for both parties. Practice the compliment sandwich.

- **Be a great coach.** Set high standards and always shoot for your partner's best efforts. Low standards are easy and comfortable but offer only an illusion of kindness. Be firm with standards that reflect a peer's true potential.

- **Critical and creative thought.** Often considered the benchmark for meaningful learning. New ideas or opinions are an asset for the greater good and offer significant payoffs for feelings of self-worth. Reflect on the feelings a critical or creative thought provides rather than the A grade or product generated. Celebrate creative or critical thought because it feels good!

NOTE. More intentions with Purpose in supplementary materials (pages 175-177).

CONNECTIONS WITH PLAY

Play is fun and full of authentic rewards helping us feel happy, healthy, and balanced. For this reason alone, setting aside time for play is a valuable endeavor, but play has benefits specific to learning itself. Many studies have shown that play significantly influences the ability to think critically and be creative. One study explains how time set aside for play before a task increases output and ideas that are more creative (Howard-Jones, Taylor, & Sutton, 2002). The research suggests play-like activities create mindsets where failing is okay, students can laugh at mistakes, and the freedom to explore and wonder dominates the experience. By removing rules or limiting constraints through play, creative insight and problem solving becomes a normal and natural way to learn. Play is a liberator of anxious mindsets.

Play is an active complex experience. It is the doing, in addition to listening, that offers the greatest benefits to brain development and learning (Wilcox, 1999). Singing and music are excellent examples of this relationship. Younger children benefit significantly with listening skills and language acquisition. Song and the rhythm of music improve memorization of material at all age levels.

Another important aspect of play is that it is nature's way to teach children they are not helpless. In his book, *Free to Learn*, Peter Gray (2013) argues that when children play free from adult interference; they truly are in control of their lives. Playful experiences allow children to make their own decisions, solve problems, create, and abide by rules that help develop social skills. They challenge themselves physically and emotionally and learn to manage acceptable levels of fear and discomfort. Like lion cubs wrestling on the savannah, children learn physicality is fun. Free play is also nature's means of helping children discover what they love.

Sample Connection Intentions for PLAY

- **Free play is fun and inspiring.** Loosen parameters of learning structures to allow room for children to freely develop and share new creative ideas.

- **Free play is emotionally balancing.** Structure time for free play for the sake of sharing healthy emotional energy.

- **Play reduces fear.** Playful energy is the enemy of fear. Sing like nobody is watching, and laugh at mistakes.

- **Encourage playful physicality.** Embrace nature's path to resilience and toughness.

NOTE. More intentions with Play in supplementary materials (page 178).

CONNECTIONS WITH PASSIONS

Passionately sing, dance, love, or explore an interest for the purpose of pleasure. Young children enthusiastically embrace their passions, but the capacity for unbridled joy is often muted as life goes by. Embracing an interest or passion is a good way to turn up the emotional volume and spice of life. It does not have to have a purpose other than joy itself. A passionate experience is training the brain how to feel really, really good.

Authentic passions are easy to identify because students feel good when they act on them. They provide healthy, emotional motivation to learn, grow, dig deeper, and persevere in the face of challenge. However, connections with passion and its closely related cousin, play, come with a caveat. They take considerably more time than traditional means of learning and cannot be rushed.

A unique passion, interest or talent is a valuable asset because it is a means to offer something nobody else can. Being and thinking different is the birthplace of creativity, innovation, and an opportunity to stretch the known world. Sometimes creativity results in a tangible product that makes an individual truly invaluable. The creative product emerging at preschool may not be world changing, but the process and practice of creative thought increases the potential for big things in the future. That is a powerful message for an insecure student who feels different.

Passion is contagious and elevates positive energy in the classroom. Students find great reward in following their unique talents or interests, but sharing them is often the ultimate reward. Unique passions and talents remain undervalued and less meaningful if not shared with others. The classroom can be a captive and willing audience.

Sample Connection Intentions for PASSIONS

- **Embrace a passion or interest purely for the sake of pleasure.** Passions trigger big, healthy emotional payoffs (endorphins) that help us rebalance.

- **Express learning or the process of learning through your favorite interest, passion, or pastime.** Art, singing, technology, drama, hobbies, and unique talents can add interest and healthy emotions to curricular objectives that may otherwise be less than inspiring.

- **Different is a good thing!** Share a unique talent, passion, or interest that nobody else can. This makes you invaluable for expanding the outlook and learning of the group. It is also a healthy way to nurture feelings of self-worth.

NOTE. More intentions with Passions in supplementary materials (page 179).

Susan Grabowski

Something's not right about Frankie

Ms. G needed some paper for a classroom project her kids were working on. While in Mr. Adams's art room, she couldn't help but notice Frankie working with intense concentration on a beautiful painting. She was taken aback somewhat, when Mr. Adams confused her further with raving reviews about Frankie's talents, work ethic, and contributions. In her class, Frankie bounced around uncontrollably. He was always off task and usually busy annoying his classmates with his incessant disruptions. She was frustrated with the amount of time and energy it took to manage the behaviors.

Susan's management strategies seemed to make no difference. She could not help but believe Frankie intentionally looked for trouble and he could never get enough of it. The incessant nagging and discipline couldn't be fun. An ADHD diagnosis made sense, but the doctors were having a tough time getting the medication just right, so she settled into the belief there was little she could do about it. Yet here the boy sat, peaceful and focused on his work. A medical diagnosis could not possibly switch on and off between classes. Clearly, his passion for art was pulling him to a better place. It wasn't drugs, teacher control, or discipline. His connection to art was simply more important and rewarding than his dysfunction. It got her thinking about other ways to take advantage of her student's hopes, passions, and needs.

CONNECTIONS WITH PRESENT THINKING

It is a rare event when true danger exists and survival mode responses are justified, but some people experience traumatic anxious feelings all the time. This is because they spend much of their time traveling to the past and future where anxiety can create any frightening story it chooses. The same freedom does not exist in the present moment because truth is the only rational story that exists in that realm.

A student cannot control the weather. In a similar way, she cannot control how others will fare against her in a competitive test or how a teacher will award a score for a particular task. All she can do is be her best at any given moment, and that means "Controlling the Controllables." We have a great deal of control over how we think and feel. This is important because the feelings or beliefs we embrace in the moment will become our behavior and ultimately our destiny. It is far more comforting to control the things we can rather than stressing about the things we cannot.

The present moment tis always more manageable and allows a person to relax and embrace personal truths that identify the best version of themselves. Mindfulness practices and recognizing anxious emotions for what they really are reduces the tendency to write an unnecessary dramatic story. Students who believe they are loved, supported, smart, and brave thrive, grow, and choose to pursue healthy behaviors. Taking time to reflect on these types of healthy beliefs and authentic truths helps students stay grounded when anxious thoughts try to take them elsewhere.

Sample Connection Intentions for PRESENT THINKING

- **Live in the present moment.** Anxiety is a time traveler. It can tell any painful story it wants in the past or future. Arm students with mindfulness strategies that help them stay grounded in Present Moment Safety. Monitor emotions and thought patterns during lessons to "check in" with the truth of the present moment.

- **Good Wolf-Evil Wolf.** The story told by the old grandfather is an excellent metaphor students of any age can use to understand true-self/false-self choices and emotional payoffs. Choosing to feed the Good Wolf is always a great intention for any lesson.

- **Control the Controllables.** Before or during a learning challenge, think about the things that may be causing you stress. Split them into matters you can and cannot control at that moment. Focus on and embrace the ones you can. You will be feeding the Good Wolf if you are successful. At the end of the task, assess how you think you did.

- **The Six Ps and personal inventories.** Use the Six Ps and personal inventory exercises to reveal a sense of authentic self. Use true-self targets to create a personalized road map leading toward health, wellness, and happiness.

NOTE. More intentions with Present Thinking in supplementary materials (pages 180-181).

 TRY THIS!

Find Your Trigger Word

When students find themselves drifting toward anxious thoughts, a personalized trigger word can help pull them back. One top international snowboarder used the word "Jell-O" to help him relax and refocus when negative thoughts crept into his mind.

Have students discover their own version of "Jell-O" to shake out the nerves.

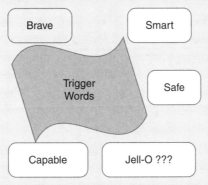

SOURCE: Contributed by Derek Winterman, 2018

CONNECTIONS WITH PERSONAL CHALLENGE AND LEARNING

Authentic connections with people, purpose, play, and passions always feel good. Personal challenge, growth, and learning are different kinds of emotional experiences. They are about risk, challenging weaknesses, explorations, and venturing into the unknown. It is the nature of true challenge and learning to be an anxious uncomfortable journey. Healthy perspectives and authentic connections can help students rebalance and celebrate their efforts.

The journey from anxious moments to more relaxed states and, on occasion, unbridled joy is exhilarating and liberating. Surviving a challenging experience is proof of resiliency, nurtures attachments to bravery, and exposes limitless boundaries for growth and learning adventure. Valuing discomfort and challenge sets the stage for growth mindsets and opens the door for meaningful shifts to unhealthy beliefs, reducing anxiety, and emotional healing.

Sample Connection Intentions for PERSONAL CHALLENGE AND LEARNING

- **Value "uncomfortable."** Plan a learning experience that triggers anxious feelings. Wrap the activity in healthy thinking patterns, support, and authentic connections to help students rebalance and celebrate their effort and growth. Classroom presentations, new social scenarios, or learning challenges with the potential for perceived failure will fit the bill.

- **Be brave.** Dive in and just do it! The first step is the one that matters most. Even if failure follows, value it. Bravery is a big deal for real learning. Think bungee jumping. Even if you hated it, embrace the fact that the bravery demonstrated in a first step is fact and can never be taken away. Answer the question even if you are not sure you have it right. Take the shot or say hello to someone new. What is the worst that can happen? Without a doubt, it is not trying.

- **Celebrate mistakes.** Value mistakes as evidence for bravery. Often it is a fear of judgment by others that makes bravery difficult. Flip the belief by making a daily intention that celebrates mistakes of classmates as a good thing.

- **Try really, really hard.** Best efforts are never easy but always worth celebrating. Testing is a valuable way to set benchmarks for task improvement or emotional growth. No fluffy compliments please—today may be the day I surprise myself with real effort and accomplishment. Grit matters.

NOTE. More intentions with Personal Challenge and Learning in supplementary materials (pages 182-183).

HOW DO I KNOW WHICH INTENTION TO USE?

The Six Ps provide an excellent reminder of ways to integrate authentic connections and healthy emotional payoffs in daily lessons, but they fall short if used as part of a fixed socioemotional agenda governed by timelines. The Six Ps are most powerful when used as strategies to fulfill the present moment needs of the class. A structured timeline works reasonably well for academic schedules and knowledge scaffolding, but a predetermined connection or attachment agenda will rarely align with a student's personal story or the current emotional climate of a particular class. This demands a closer look at the narrative each student brings to the classroom.

"Getting to know you" activities or true-self type exercises that expose the types of attachments students bring to the classroom are useful because they start the process of thinking about authentic wants and feelings. An introspection of lifestyles and authentic wants creates targets teachers and students can use to begin building a believable true-self story. Mind maps or personal posters can work in a similar way. However, the response can often be superficial. Unhealthy attachments to shame, anger, or guilt are sneaky and will hide and linger beneath the surface. Teachers will usually need to direct probing questions to help reveal a student's authentic truth.

My Greatest Wants	My Authentic Wants
• Family	"I am":
• To play pro football	• Love, family, belonging
• Close friends	• Contribution
• Lots of money	• Learning and growing
• Good grades	• Sports
• Prestigious career	• Nature and environment
• Fame	
• Be cool	
• Save the whales	
• Facebook supremacy	

True Self Exercise

- Fold a piece of paper in half. Brainstorm your greatest wants in life.
- Pick the five wants you feel are most important to you. This is your authentic self.

Question: Does your daily life and learning align with your authentic wants?

INTENTIONS: A POWERFUL DIAGNOSTIC TOOL FOR EMOTIONAL WELLNESS

Daily connection intentions are the best way to get to know your class because only real experiences reveal real attachments. In effect, they serve as a test of emotional attachments. If a lesson focus and assessment is on bravery, cooperation, challenge, or connection skills, it is incredibly revealing. The emotional and behavioral response will identify strengths to exploit and weaknesses to challenge. Real experiences provide the most powerful diagnostic tool for emotional wellness or dysfunction. Anxiety will have difficulty hiding.

> *Daily intentions and assessment are the best diagnostic tools a teacher has to reveal the attachments a child brings to the classroom.*

When a student struggles with an intention that should feel good, it raises an obvious red flag that a curricular-focused teaching model misses. Invariably, the most disconnected will have the greatest anxious response. The behavior or emotional coping strategy may be minor and something a teacher can manage in his class, or it may necessitate notification to parents or a counselor. In severe or chronic cases, the red flag may be a really big one.

THINK ABOUT IT

In a world of teen suicide, mental illness, and school shootings, a connection-focused educational model may save lives. Teachers can see real experiences and emotions in action that a psychologist could never see.

Teachers are observational experts who can read the landscape and determine the emotional needs of the class with incredible accuracy. There is no right or wrong when it comes to selecting and setting daily intentions. They will nurture a healthy attachment or expose an unhealthy one. Both outcomes are important and valuable for a natural balanced learning experience. The more frequent daily intentions are set and assessed the quicker teachers will get to know the long-term wellness and learning needs in their classroom.

Shakespeare: Setting Intentions—A Case Study

Ms. Watt, a young teacher in training, had the task of setting connection intentions for the upcoming Shakespeare unit in her English 10 class. Before her was a classic piece of literature, but she was unsure that the story and unusual language would resonate with her students. She began her undertaking by thinking about the Six Ps. What could *Romeo and Juliet* offer in terms of healthy thought patterns and emotional payoffs? By definition, *Romeo and Juliet* is a tragedy, so naturally the highest-level intention that came to mind revolved around critically examining and thinking about trauma, processing painful emotions, and resiliency. Learning to deal with trauma by means of an emotionally explicit dramatic fictional piece would certainly represent a connected intention with lifelong benefits.

However, she quickly realized there were several roadblocks that she, and more specifically her students, had to overcome for an emotionally meaningful experience to occur. A high percentage of her students were English second language, and as a collective whole, they could be described as a low-motivation group who typically avoided peer connection and engaging conversation in favor of independent seatwork they were more comfortable with. She decided to embrace these challenges as an opportunity for growth, and Romeo and Juliet were going to help her. The unit would culminate with a passionate oral debate about tragedy, healthy thinking, and resiliency. But first, she had to set the stage with a few connection intentions to help her students embrace the challenge. Understandably, students were a little nervous. She set up her connection intention with a promise.

"It feels great to share critical thoughtful opinions that help others understand or view things in new ways. Sharing what we think or know is one way we bring value to the collective whole, and to ourselves. This might sound scary to some, but I promise if you dive in and are brave enough to share your thoughts, it will feel amazing."

Over the 2-week unit, she set up the following daily connection intentions. A self-assessment at the end of each lesson measured their feelings and commitment to the connection objection.

- Be brave and fearless. There is no right or wrong with opinion; value taking risk, just dive in, and share your thoughts.

- Share your ideas with enthusiasm. Be interesting, share healthy energy, and attract the attention you deserve. Use eye contact, volume, animation, and body posture.

- Be vulnerable and embrace the passion. *Romeo and Juliet* is all about emotion—joyful and painful. Project yourself into the story and critically think about working through the emotions in healthy ways.

It took time and encouragement from teacher and peers alike, but a significant shift in the emotional energy of the class occurred. The debate was a lively affair of free-flowing, passionate opinions. As she had hoped, her students had read and critically examined the story of Romeo and Juliet, but it was the smiles, personalities, and expressive emotions she found most exciting. Ms. Watt was certain, in the most literal sense, the learning experience changed the hearts and minds of her students for the better. The Good Wolf was well fed.

 TRY THIS!

Be an Enthusiastic Cheerleader!

Forget the cartwheels and challenging dance moves. An enthusiastic cheerleader combines many complex connection skills. Take a week and introduce a new skill each day during your regular lessons.

- **Monday:** Turn up the volume. Teach students to project their voice from the diaphragm. The challenge this poses for some students is surprising.

- **Tuesday:** Body posture. Practice engaged body posture and facial expressions that show interest during peer conversations and learning.

- **Wednesday:** Animation. Use hand gestures and movement to communicate. Try a game of charades to demonstrate key points of your lesson.

- **Thursday:** Compliment skills. Learn positive words and practice making a compliment sandwich when coaching a new skill to a peer.

- **Friday:** Healthy thinking patterns. Recognize that anxiety hates unbridled enthusiasm and it will always create stories to hold a student back. Reflect on the emotions experienced during the week. The good ones felt great, and the anxious ones were uncomfortable. Make a choice—embrace authentic and free!

Every student truly wants to be the personable classmate with the enthusiastic charm that draws others in, but they may lack the skills to do so. Anxiety complicates matters further because it attempts to create stories that say it is an impossibility and a task better suited to others. Simple skills like learning to speak loudly can be a symbolic representation of bravery for a repressed shy student. Shoulders back, chest out, and speak loudly from the diaphragm in a lower register. The task is easily identifiable and measurable as completed or not. The simplicity of the task takes the thinking out of letting go and embracing bravery. Success of less complex tasks proves connection is possible. Being a great cheerleader is an excellent way to liberate healthy emotions impaired by anxiety or weak connection skill sets.

ALIGNING EDUCATION, CONTENT OBJECTIVES, AND CONNECTION INTENTIONS

It is hard to imagine anything more important than learning to live a life aligned with healthy thoughts, behaviors, and feelings. When teachers are free to "walk the talk," they are at their best. When faced with daily curricular and administrative pressures, best intentions can be left behind. For example, a teacher may proclaim that he values mistakes, but when report cards come around, test scores tell another story. The pressures of fitting in course content can get in the way of time needed for emotional alignment intentions. It is not his fault; it is the consequence of the very real pressures of an antiquated system.

The goal of a connection intention is not about doing or learning things well. It is about experiencing healthy emotions during and after the learning process. This is how learning, healthy beliefs, and emotional balance come together.

Traditional learning outcomes influence what a student learns, and connection intentions influence how they experience the learning. They work best together, and beliefs that they compete for time are unfounded. Certainly, connection skills will have to be front-loaded, but eventually authentic connection becomes a natural part of the learning experience. Integrating authentic connection intentions is advantageous to traditional learning outcomes because

- Pleasurable experiences and feelings are attached to curriculum that may be less than inspiring to some students

- Emotionally balanced students are ready to learn, be challenged, and perform

- Intrinsic motivation is always grounded in the emotional payoffs of healthy connections

- Motivated students need less supervision

- Traditional test scores will improve

- They are a powerful diagnostic tool for emotional wellness

If a student is not experiencing healthy emotions during learning, it is a certainty unhealthy ones are present. The Bad Wolf does not need anxiety or emotional distress for its food. He is more than happy to embrace and feed on boredom or no emotion at all. Passively neglecting the healthy connected payoffs we need to survive will always lead to emotional distress and imbalance. This is why an active intention to infuse healthy emotions is so important to the learning process.

Connected experiences always end in rewarding feelings that make us feel good or feel better. That in itself is a worthy reason to embrace connections, but feelings have repercussions that reach much further than a quick emotional payoff and/or a feel-good lesson. Feelings have a profound effect on belief systems, brain chemistry, and healthy attachments setting the course for life ahead. Targeting and assessing emotional reward may be the most important educational intention. Feelings create belief, belief governs behavior, and ultimately behavior will determine one's destiny. That is a big deal! The next chapter takes a closer look at how feelings, healthy or unhealthy, play an incredibly important role in emotional attachment processes and brain development.

Johnny

Isolation and Emotional Addiction

A gentle breeze cut the heat of the beautiful sunny day. Groups of students laughed and played as they made their way down the tree-lined street. There was every reason to be happy, but Johnny just didn't feel that way. Once again, he was walking home from school alone, and the gleeful squeals of the other kids added to his agitation. Johnny clenched his teeth and quickened his pace. There was a time when he was one of them. As he cut through the grounds of the local community center, pleasant memories of his time as a boy scout made him wonder why he quit. The challenges he faced with his fellow scouts were so much fun. He tried to convince himself that he quit because it just wasn't cool, but he knew that was a lie.

He opened the door to his home and made his way straight to his room. Piles of clothes littered the floor, and dishes with crusted-on food from last night's partially eaten dinner lay beside his game controller. The boy navigated his way through the mess, pushed aside the dishes, and turned on the game console. The stress of the day melted away with pings and pangs of the game. The killing felt good, and he drifted off to the place that made him feel safe. Hours later, fatigue set in and he turned off the game. A fresh plate of food sat at his side, but he went to sleep without eating, feeling more alone than ever.

Johnny's Mother

Desperate Love

She wanted nothing more than a normal, happy life and worked hard to make her home comfortable for her family, but despite her efforts, the tension never seemed to lift. Walking on eggshells around Johnny was the way of things when he was home, and her anxiety only worsened the moment he stepped out the door for school. She loved her child and desperately worried about his sadness and his seemingly endless confrontations at school. At least when he was in his room she knew he wouldn't get into too much trouble. Anything could happen at school, and that frightened her deeply.

The smell of Johnny's favorite cookies baking in the oven filled the kitchen. She sat at the table as she often did, flipping through the family photo album. Smiling faces reminded her of happier times and triggered tiny flickers of hope of what could be again. It was one of the few ways she could find the energy to continue on. The child in the photos was beautiful, kind, and happy. She carefully made her way through the pages in a desperate attempt to spot the moment when the transformation happened.

The answer eluded her just as it had every other day, and she slammed the cover in frustration. Johnny had slowly disappeared into another world she didn't understand.

The only peace he seemed to grasp was in his room, alone with his television and video games. She knew this was a problem, but interrupting his alone time was met with uncontrollable outbursts of anger that seemed beyond her control. Despite her efforts, his sadness and depression only deepened. Counseling didn't seem to help, and antidepression drugs prescribed by the doctor just seemed to numb him further. This was not the lovely boy in the photo album, and it broke her heart that she was unable to protect him from the pain that refused to leave him. They were caring parents who had tried everything, and it didn't make sense. Tears of frustration and sadness trickled down her cheek.

CHAPTER 3

Experiences, Emotions, Attachments, and Scary Kittens

I love math. I loved my teacher, Ms. Grabowski. These beliefs are a product of a learning experience and the joyful meaningful emotions that accompanied it.

I hate science, and Mr. Jones was a jerk! This less favorable belief is also a product of emotions, but they may not necessarily be a reflection of truth. Mr. Jones may indeed be a jerk, but it is also possible he is a very competent, kind, and caring teacher. Emotions do not have to align with truth to have very real consequences. This disconnection is how unhealthy attachments are often reinforced. For the chronically disconnected child, anxious feelings create false stories that become their reality.

In either scenario, what is undeniable is that an emotional attachment has shaped a belief. Neural adaptations and connectivity hardwire the link, and Mr. Jones will remain a jerk until a new experience or thought pattern emotes a feeling powerful enough to rewrite the story.

FEELINGS ARE A REAL THING

It might be easy to dismiss the passionate cries of an infant in mild discomfort, a child frightened by a tiny kitten, or a teen distressed by hallway drama. The moment is fleeting and soon things will settle. A truthful perspective suggests the emotions were unnecessary anyway. The infant had gas, a kitten poses no real danger, and teen drama is often far larger than it needs to be. Nonetheless, all feelings are a physiological reality and may come with lasting consequences. Healthy or not, truthful or unnecessary, emotions influence brain chemistry and neural development. They shape who we are and give context for future experiences.

Feelings are a complex interaction and expression of hormones, neural circuitry, thought patterns, and experiences. The brain's limbic system acts as a pattern recognition network responsible for organizing memories and events in your life. This neural circuitry influences perceptions, attitudes, and feelings that determine how present moment experiences unfold. In turn, each new experience and associated set of emotions adds to or modifies existing neural pathways and patterns. This is especially true if the emotions are particularly powerful or frequent. These patterns represent emotional attachments that significantly influence whether or any particular future experience triggers feelings of joy or emotional pain.

Neural network patterns will influence how children perceive events. Trauma or disconnected experiences may result in neural dysregulations that strengthen unhealthy attachments and thought patterns. A kitten is scary if attachments and the emotional story say it is.

EMOTIONAL ATTACHMENTS

Attachments are a neurological representation of the emotional bond with people, objects, beliefs, or behaviors. Connected feelings and experiences support balanced emotional states and neural circuitry that nurture normal attachment processes. The more frequent a healthy emotional neural activation occurs, the more influential the attachment or belief becomes (Barker, n.d.).

Happy people are annoyingly happy all the time because their neural networks align with connected experiences and thought patterns that supply them with a constant stream of healthy endorphin payoffs. When things do not go exactly as planned, they easily rebound and continue on their merry way through life. Somehow, they find a way, even in their most uncomfortable moments, to uncover feelings of safety and joy. The cup half-full attitude is a product of previous experiences, thought patterns, and feelings. Connected moments and feelings have built a neural template aligned with happiness.

The hunter-gatherer theme is valuable because it reminds us of the link between our physiology and the need for connection. Connectedness remains a necessary biological truth that plays a key role in the lifelong process of healthy attachment acquisition. Chronic disconnection from authentic connections has the opposite effect. Our hunter-gatherer brain and physiology will always interpret disconnection as a threat worthy of survival mode emotions. For children lacking connected experiences needed for normal development, attachments to love, safety, bravery, self-worth, or adventure are an unlikely scenario. They become stuck in a perpetual state of emotional pain. The resulting neural template solidifies an emotionally imbalanced condition causing a snowball like effect for painful experiences in the future.

Safety and Early Attachments

When adults experience an event, they have existing background to pull from. They process or filter the experience through the lens of their existing attachments and fully developed cognitive skill sets. They react or alter their behavior accordingly to cope with the scenario. Things are quite different for young children facing new experiences.

The human brain is incredibly complex, but the general rule of thumb is simple. What you put in is what you get out. This is especially important in infancy where the social areas of the brain are relatively undeveloped and highly responsive to their senses and connected loving experiences. The more rewarding social experiences a baby has, the more this part of the brain develops (Gerhardt, 2004). Trauma or neglect, as in the case of the neglected Romanian orphan studies, will lead to underdevelopment of the social parts of the brain.

A child's brain, relatively speaking, is a blank slate, and the only context he may have is the immediate senses and emotion directly linked to any particular experience. Young children and infants in particular, are remarkably attuned to the emotional energy and sensory experiences their caregivers provide. Their brain is like a sponge, seeking context to help process new adventures and the surrounding world. It is receptive to loving feelings and support. The drive for sensory context also leaves children vulnerable to anxious emotions others consciously or unconsciously share.

Assuming things go according to plan during pregnancy, children come into the world programmed to embrace healthy connections. They are depending on a loving parent–child experience for feelings of safety and comfort that lay the foundation for healthy attachments to follow. When these critical early attachments go well, neural circuitry stays true with nature's plan for expectations related to feelings of safety, joy, and love. When things inevitably get challenging or uncomfortable, these attachments will be available to help pull them back to a place of emotional safety. Children with poorly formed safety and connection attachments may have to manage life's challenges without this important resiliency tool.

Beyond infancy, neural connections slow and it becomes more of a "use it or lose it" scenario, but still the brain remains flexible throughout life and continues to produce new neural pathways and emotional attachments as older, unused pathways weaken. Most socioemotional initiatives at school focus on early grade experiences. This is a defendable "most bang for the buck" way of thinking because emotional attachments occur more frequently at this time.

Credit goes to grade school philosophy and practices. The teachers think a lot about emotional safety and wellness and work hard to create optimal conditions for happy learners and healthy attachments. However, as the years progress, socioemotional considerations and the attachments that come with them become a lessening priority in the presence of growing curricular demands. Outside of school, increasing screen time and diminishing connections with family and natural play with friends, right or wrong, means that a large proportion of the experiences children need for normal attachment acquisition and maintenance will have to happen at school. If school culture lacks significant connection objectives and opportunities, the *lose it* scenario becomes a concern. Again, in the absence of healthy emotional payoffs, connections to unhealthy ones are almost a certainty. At a time when curricular pressures may be at their greatest, the emotional balance students need for wellness and healthy beliefs may be a neglected entity.

> *"The brain changes not only from what you do, but also from what you do not do."*
> —Laura Boyd, UBC Brain Researcher (2015)

THE NATURE OF EDUCATION AND LEARNING

Brain development and the act of creating, strengthening, and discarding neural connections is, in effect, the nuts and bolts of learning. Attachment acquisition is like much of the curricular structures that takes place at school; new attachments are dependent on prior experiences. Early safety attachments lay the foundation for more complex attachments that help children navigate the challenge of curricular and more complex social experiences ahead. It is the hope of classroom teachers that early safety attachments have been successful. High rates of child anxiety in early grades and greater yet in high school may suggest they have not.

> *"The proportion of young people reporting frequent feelings of depression or anxiety doubled between the mid-80s and mid-2000s to 2 in 30 for boys and 1 in 10 for girls."*
>
> *(Collishaw, Maughan, Natarajan, & Pickles, 2010)*

Nonetheless, the brain remains resilient, and although it may be challenging, new experiences, thought patterns, and rewarding emotional payoffs can rework neural connections that push children toward emotional distress. This is an advantage that teachers have in their pocket. Emotion is the key ingredient for attachment formation or healing, and the educational experience is full of it!

Learning and social challenge demands exploration, risk, and difficulty. All these experiences can be uncomfortable and emotionally charged. Left unchecked, attachments to lingering painful emotions are a realistic possibility, and the risk that students make a link between emotional pain and learning is high. Those who come to school with existing dysfunctional attachments and weak connections are the most vulnerable of all.

It is safe to make one of two assumptions about children in the classroom. They will be bringing anxious emotional attachments with them, or they will be experiencing anxious emotions as part of the normal learning process. Either way, the educational or therapeutic intention remains the same: training the brain to cope with the challenge by making the shift from a state of dysregulation to regulation, anxiety to balance, dysfunctional thought patterns to connection, and, most important, emotional pain to joy.

Training the Brain: Be a Great Coach

Great coaches know that learning, growth, and improvement come with the price of uncomfortable feelings. They teach athletes to accept this as normal and even celebrate it. Athletes stress their bodies to the point of physical pain with the expectation they will respond, adapt, and recover, stronger and more skilled than ever. True competitors learn to value discomfort because it is associated with the satisfying feelings of improvement. They leave exhausting training sessions feeling good about what they have done.

Physical improvements and skill sets are not the only modifications that occur during training. An athlete's brain has also experienced change. Facing and overcoming fears, weaknesses, and unhealthy thought patterns has also left its mark on neural circuitry. Repetition of the uncomfortable emotionally taxing process is what liberates athletes from the unhealthy attachments and thinking patterns that inhibit best effort performances: emotional neural dysregulation and rebalancing—over and over again. They become wired to emotionally recover from anything.

The process of preparing for the unpredictability and difficulties of competition is taxing and often rides the line of emotional breaking points. Cross the line too far or too often, unhealthy attachments emerge and the athlete loses love for sport and quits. Great coaches have an emotional training plan. They do not obsess about winning; they target healthy attachments and lifelong takeaways. They know their athletes, identify when they struggle, adjust the game plan, and intuitively offer support when needed.

Emotional and Experiential Alignment

The curricular or content part of learning is relatively easy. In traditional pedagogical thinking, teachers teach and students learn a sequentially crafted measurable list of ideas, concepts, skills, and tasks. To a far less degree, socioemotional learning targets exist, but they often remain vague add-ons that are difficult to measure and may not necessarily align with the present moment attachment needs of children. The challenge becomes greater yet when teachers attempt to deliver socioemotional objectives in the same way they teach curriculum. Healthy emotional attachments are not taught. They are the product of emotional experiences. This is how connection or attachment intentions differ from curricular ones.

Emotional attachments are the product of rewarding emotional experiences. This is the core purpose of the Six Ps and connection intentions.

Shakespeare's *Romeo and Juliet*

Connection Intentions—Share your ideas with enthusiasm: be interesting, share healthy energy and attract the attention you deserve. Use eye contact, volume, animation, and body posture.

Curricular Objective—Critically explore the core themes of *Romeo and Juliet*.

Educational strategies and learning experiences should align with the needs and readiness of students. Infants grow into children, and teens into young adults ready to take on the challenges of the world. At each stage of development, they have to rely on experiences provided to nurture authentic healthy attachments. As children mature, beliefs that support independence, friendships, contribution, passions, resiliency, and healthy intimate relationships are always evolving and require an environment where experiences align with attachment needs.

Managing the emotions of children and engineering attachments may seem like a daunting task for the already overworked teacher, but if teachers think about their best ever lesson, it was not because of the curriculum. In some way, they created an experience that triggered endorphin rewards supporting a feel-good learning experience that just may also have nudged the disconnected a little closer toward emotional balance and healthy beliefs. What could be more rewarding than that?

GROWTH MINDSET, HOPE, AND NEUROSCIENCE: IT'S KID STUFF!

At every educational level, students are emotionally ready to learn or they are not. The question for students and teachers alike is if this is a fixed condition for those that are not. What would be the point in trying if this was true? Carol Dweck's (2006) Growth Mindset research suggests it is possible for performance, learning capacity, and even intelligence to improve with hard work and healthy perspectives toward failure and grit. This is a hopeful perspective for students hamstrung by anxious emotions and beliefs that tell them they cannot achieve and grow.

Children managing life with false self-beliefs and emotions feel hopeless and stuck. They don't believe in their capacity to obtain the kind of future they may truly want. They believe they are what they are, intellectually, emotionally, and spiritually, but this just isn't true. They are the product of experiences, but experiences can change with knowledge, perspective, and hope. Even young children can understand the connection between neural pathways and the experiential pathways of life. Knowledge tells them how to set goals and own the experiences that can change their brains in healthy ways. Knowledge opens the door of possibility. Hope provides the motivation. Experience creates tangible change.

At home and school, children are taught about their body parts and how most things work, but the most important part, the brain, the part that manages pretty much everything, is usually passed by with the belief it is too complex for meaningful understanding. Children do not have to be neuroscientists, they just have to be competent users of basic knowledge and believe that change is possible.

Ms. Grabowski

Neural Pathways, Learning, and Happiness

Here is a big number. Approximately 100 billion nerve cells called neurons exist in your brain. When you are using your brain or experiencing something, electrical signals pass from neuron to neuron. These signals cannot just go anywhere. That would be a mess.

Instead, chemical messengers called neurotransmitters cross a tiny gap called a synapse with receptors on the next neuron acting like a gate. If the gate opens, the electrical signal is free to move onto the next neuron. Now here is the important part. When the gate consistently opens and a neural path is travelled often, it gets stronger and signals travel faster. This is basically how we remember things and learn. Lots of strong pathways mean that we can remember more and learn things easier. One person isn't really smarter than the next. One person just may have more well-used pathways or connections that make some things seem easier for them. Anybody can get smarter with practice and learning.

Susan paused for a moment to let them think about.

Here's another thing I want you to consider. We all want to be smarter, but we may also want to be braver, athletic, more social, or even happier. Make a choice, it is not that complicated. Experiences shape who we are, and each experience lays down neural pathways that bring you closer to your goal. The more fun experiences you have the easier it is to be fun all the time. If the fun pathway becomes well-worn, eventually you travel it without even thinking about being happy.

On that note, I just learned a really fun anatomy game we can play together.

Johnny wanted to be happy, but it seemed too easy and, if anything, the lesson made him feel mad and resentful.

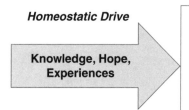

Homeostatic Drive

Knowledge, Hope, Experiences

Ms. Grabowski covered all the bases. Knowledge, hope, and connected experiences work with the body's natural homeostatic drive to nurture healthy beliefs and a healthy happy brain.

The shift from a fixed mindset to one of growth is dependent on knowledge, hope, and a changing belief system. In turn, a shift in belief is dependent on an emotional experience to prove it is possible. This is when things can get tricky. Existing unhealthy emotional attachments and established neural pathways will always create a pull in another direction. When setting an intention to create a connected experience, the presence of existing unhealthy or weak attachments that may act as roadblocks must be a first consideration. Challenging them is never a comfortable endeavor.

Immersing children in connected, feel-good experiences is a good thing. Most attachments are a product of emotional payoffs related to people, purpose, play, and passions. Unfortunately, this is just one piece of the puzzle. Life is a struggle. Growth and change are a struggle. Every new adventure, learning experience, and social interaction comes with some degree of emotional risk and the potential for tears. Growing is a by-product of emotional discomfort and good old-fashioned hard work. A growth mindset recognizes and celebrates this. Moving forward means accepting this as normal and not obsessing about discomfort in negative ways. A healthy perspective will embrace uncomfortable experiences and emotions as the most powerful opportunity of all for meaningful change. Even though it is difficult, growth or overcoming an emotional roadblock always feels good no matter how uncomfortable the process was.

Embracing Uncomfortable

Long-time preschool teacher Kathy Geremia was all about fun and healthy energy, but her sense that anxiety and dysfunctional behaviors in her classroom were on the rise discomforted her. Despite their best efforts at the award-winning preschool, participation was often a struggle, and the occasional social skirmish ended in anger, hitting, or tears. One of the greatest challenges seemed to be the drop-off period. Separation anxiety was a growing concern for children and parents alike.

Free play was one of the strategies implemented to reduce anxious emotions at drop off. Four different activities were set up, allowing children to choose stations where they felt most comfortable. Results were nominal for the children with the greatest challenges, and chronic anxious emotions continued to affect behavior throughout the day.

Kathy had recently come across The Emotionally Connected Classroom model, and one of the flaws she noticed in the strategy they were using was that children were always choosing activities with which they were most comfortable. They were at a place of learning, but children predominantly pursued what they already knew and found comfortable. Engagement during free time remained remarkably void of authentically rewarding peer connections, learning challenges, adventure, or emotional joy. Yes, they were comfortable, but in effect, it was a nonevent, incapable of changing thought patterns and emotional states. It was time for challenge and some healthy endorphin payoffs.

Comfortable was no longer an option or objective. Teachers sent students to stations they felt would be challenging and stimulating. Children worked in pairs and were encouraged to use strategies to support each other. There were some initial emotional protests at first. It was more difficult for some than others, especially those with social challenges. At first, Kathy questioned the strategy. Watching children struggle was difficult, but she stayed the course. To her relief, students soon embraced the new way of business. Children worked together and supported each other, and new friendships emerged. It was clear that social connections, challenge, and purpose were changing the emotional landscape. One parent was both startled and overjoyed by his child's new love for spelling. Another was amazed that her unusually shy daughter would sing in front of a group. Sometimes children need a little push into the world of "uncomfortable." It is not a bad place at all.

Nice Versus Kind

Nurturing comfortable environments and learning experiences is a nice thing to do. It is also the easy part of teaching because there is no risk. Pushing children toward uncomfortable feelings is far more work. It demands anticipation of existing unhealthy attachments, frontloading connections, emotional preparation, and support strategies. It is difficult to watch children struggle. Kind teachers are willing to accept this fact and join their students on the journey from the discomfort of emotional challenge to joy.

SAFETY, CHALLENGE, AND TRUTH

A pervasive cultural obsession with safety attachments and do no harm philosophies has taken hold in early child rearing practices that limit emotional risk, challenge, and the potential for failure. "Everybody gets a ribbon" sends a mixed message. The purpose of valuing everybody is clear, but an extrinsic reward given for what may have been a noneffort is confusing. Self-esteem initiatives grounded in never-fail perspectives can create their own set of dangers. The exclusivity of activities that target comfortable feelings does not reflect a balanced approach for future realities. The focus is often on either eliminating or managing anxious emotions rather than tackling the unhealthy attachments that drive them. In extreme cases, absolute protection strategies may be their own form of emotional abuse because they steal a child's opportunity to take risks, embrace bravery, and forge resiliency attachments critical for meaningful learning and growth. In the coming years, they will be facing unavoidable stress and be left unarmed.

Young children are surprisingly intuitive, and the necessity of emotional protection on the part of adults suggests children should fear and avoid challenge. If a social, performance, or physical task is set aside for reasons of perceived safety, no experience has occurred and all that remains are the fearful stories anxiety creates. The nontask is more frightening than ever, and a reinforcement of fear attachments may occur. This is the most problematic aspect of protection-avoidance strategies. Fear or anxiety that is not processed will never go away and may even escalate as the stories created become far more dramatic than any real-life experience that may actually occur. An appropriately challenging task with frontloading and support gives context and an opportunity to process a manageable amount of discomfort.

The "monster under the bed" is a powerful and frightening reality. Until a child actively faces the discomfort of her fear, takes a look, and experiences a truthful present moment reality, her thinking patterns will not change. Anxiety would suggest the child wait it out through a long, emotionally painful night.

By the time students get to high school, the emotional protection umbrella is largely cast aside with the expectation that mature students are resilient and can handle more. Well-meaning but token socioemotional efforts in senior grades pale in comparison to the constant barrage of curricular and social challenges students face. Teachers stretched by curricular demands and limited time to build connections struggle to know the emotional needs of their students. What remains is a sink-or-swim educational approach for students to navigate largely unaided.

Under normal conditions, life-threating scenarios at school should be a nonfactor, but the cumulative effect of curricular and social challenges can often feel traumatic. The biggest drawback to the sink-or-swim approach is that stressed out students with nominal healthy connections and resiliency attachments will not be able to rebalance from a stressful sink outcome. Linking their enduring emotional pain with education, learning, and social interactions is a probable outcome.

The upside of the sink-or-swim approach is that it mirrors the realities of the competitive, disconnected world they will soon enter. Students will have the opportunity to sort out social challenges, winning, losing, and uncomfortable feelings. The successful competitors acquire attachments that reflect growth and confidence. Those who manage to process their perceived failures in healthy ways may discover they are resilient and failure is not the end of the world. They may even use the experience for motivation to try harder. Still, this best-case, sink-or-swim scenario will contain losers traumatized by the experience (see Figure 3.1).

FIGURE 3.1

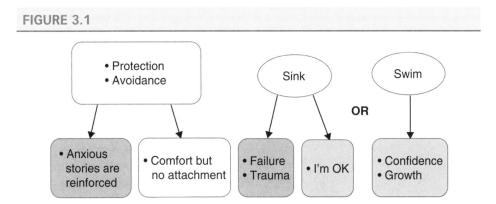

Instinctually, a protection-avoidance strategy is a better attachment acquisition option, but a closer look suggests otherwise. Still, leaving attachment to chance is really no strategy at all.

ATTACHMENT INTENTIONS

A better way to forge healthy attachments in a consistent manner is to reduce the element of chance. A more predictable outcome begins with an understanding that emotions, pleasurable or uncomfortable, are the pivot point for attachments that dictate who a child becomes. Authentic connected feelings help us through difficult times. Uncomfortable ones are a product of stretching, growing, and resilience. Even chronic unhealthy emotions have value. They expose unhealthy attachments and give us a precise target for connection intentions and emotional healing. Emotions of all kinds are a teacher's most valuable tool. The ability to assess, adapt, and manipulate the emotional energy surrounding the learning experience in a positive way is the foundational piece in the art of teaching.

Emotional baggage and the stressful nature of the educational system makes it a challenge to stay ahead of unhealthy emotions. Left unchecked, fear, anger, shame, and loneliness will always lead to dysfunctional thoughts and behaviors that make life worse and distance children from truthful perspectives. This is why beginning lessons with connection intentions that support the emotional learning experience with connection strategies is so important.

Sometimes teachers and parents appear to do everything right, and things still go wrong. They create connected environments and offer challenging joyful experiences, but some children just do not bite. Why would a child refuse to engage in a wonderful authentic learning opportunity that should make them feel good? This seemingly complex question has a simple explanation. There is a lot of competition for the beliefs, emotions, and feelings of children. Knowing what teachers and children are up against is an excellent starting point for an effective connectedness intervention. The next chapter examines the modern-day forces that compete for dominance over our children's attention.

Johnny

The Test

Nervous energy permeated throughout the quiet classroom. Mr. Jones dropped the test face down on Johnny's desk and moved on to the next. Johnny had every intention of studying, but once again, he allowed himself to be caught up gaming into the late hours of the evening. Now it was time to pay the price. He failed the last test, and his parents were not happy. They took his games away for a week. His heart began to race. He noticed the pencil gently trembling in his hand.

"You have forty minutes. Turn over your papers and begin."

Johnny flipped over his test and glanced at the first few questions. He had every reason to panic. He answered what questions he could, but his pencil soon fell silent as the others continued to scratch away. He couldn't bare the shame and disappointment of another failure.

Mr. Jones had settled into work at his desk. Johnny didn't feel good about it, but cheating seemed to be his only answer. Besides, if Mr. Jones were a better teacher he would not have to cheat. He turned toward Alice and furiously began scribbling answers until she noticed and covered her paper.

"Bitch."

Bobby to his left wasn't as smart, but his answers would do. He once again began to jot down answers until a sense of unease forced his head to rise. Mr. Jones was looking straight at him. He dropped his head to feign working on his own. His worries rose with the scrape of a chair sliding back. The echo of footsteps down the side of the class ended directly behind his desk. He was certain he could feel the breath and angry glare of Mr. Jones on the back of his head.

His mind raced with stories of a raging teacher, the walk to the principal's office, and worst of all, the disappointment of his parents, but nothing happened. The silence was excruciating as his teacher just sat there for the remainder of the test. It was agonizing. When the bell finally rang, Mr. Jones asked the class to leave papers on their desk and then just walked away.

Johnny didn't know what to think or feel. He probably had enough answers to pass. He should have been relieved and happy that he had dodged a bullet, but he didn't feel that way. His shame was unbearable as he exited the classroom so he switched to his more familiar feelings of anger.

"Mr. Jones is a jerk-off!" Over the next few days he made sure he told it to everybody who would listen. He hated the feelings getting caught had caused him. He swore he would get better at cheating for next time.

Mr. Jones

Mr. Jones felt disappointed and deflated. He had hoped his extra efforts with Johnny would have helped. He couldn't just let the boy cheat, but he knew Johnny had a lot going on and he didn't want to stress him further. It was only a test. Still, he had to send a message, so he walked to the back of the class and continued his marking. He could feel Johnny's nervous energy, and he decided that was punishment enough. Maybe he could make up for it with a retest in a week or two. Perhaps he should have talked with Johnny to ease his worries before he let him leave the class.

CHAPTER 4

Where Did My True Self Go?

Children come into the world wired to embrace love, family, purpose, and possess an instinctive drive to learn and grow in unique directions. Laughing, playing, and enthusiastically sharing their emotions are the natural state of things. They value and freely celebrate who they are. As children age and grow, connectedness increasingly becomes a challenge, and as anxiety levels escalate, the effects on health, wellness, and learning become a growing concern.

Up to one in five adolescents experience a mental disorder at some time. An estimated $247 billion is spent annually on childhood mental disorders.

—U.S. National Research Council and Institute of Medicine report (2009; adapted from Eisenberg & Neighbors, 2007)

Linking disconnection directly with this shocking statistic is difficult. This is at least in part because of inconsistent definitions among varying fields of study. However, documentation of the link between anxiety and a wide range of physical and emotional health issues is significant (Harvard Health Publishing, 2018). Rates of anxiety and depression among youth have been on the rise for the last fifty years. Almost all the available evidence suggests a sharp rise in anxiety, depression, and mental health issues among western youth between the early twentieth century and the early 1990s (Twenge, 2011). Some estimate five to eight times as many high schoolers meet the criteria for anxiety or depression as did their predecessors from the first half of the last century.

WHERE DO WE GO WRONG?

All children need love, security, and guidance to develop the traits and true-self potential they were born to embrace. It does not happen all on its own. In a perfect world, supportive parents dial in on their children's gifts and provide the necessary support and encouragement that enable them to explore, take risks, and pursue their passions. As children grow, schools share in this responsibility. If all goes well, the young adult will graduate with a strong sense of self that remains authentic and true. Individual passions blossom as they mature into great writers, doctors, dancers, and artists. This all sounds very simple, so where do we go wrong?

As children age, disconnecting pressures seem to multiply and mute natural authentic connections. Relationships with those they love appear to become less important, their sense of purpose diminishes, and personal passions are set aside for less authentic behaviors, pursuits, and cheap extrinsic reward. The result is emotionally anxious students suffering from a wide range of health and wellness issues that complicate the struggle to thrive and learn.

These same pressures make parenting and educating more difficult than they have ever been. Raising children was much less confusing for the hunter-gatherer. Life was simple. There were no televisions, video games, or smart phones to distract children from healthy connections with their family and friends. The constant bombardment of false messages prioritizing designer clothes, fancy cars, personal image, unhealthy sex, drugs, and violence just did not exist. There were not a lot of options other than play, contribute, love, and connect. They were happy and needed little more than one another.

Historically speaking, the world has become a safer place for youth. Increasing wealth and support services have made access to food and shelter a nonfactor for most children. Advances in health care have increased our ability to treat or even prevent major illnesses. Forward thinking addressing the social injustices of race, gender, or sexual orientation has given hope to youth trapped by their own identity. Bullying is at the forefront of every school's cultural agenda. In spite of significant progress with these very real issues, anxiety remains on the rise.

Modern-Day Disconnection

Modern day disconnections are diverse, and no two students experience them in the same way. The only certainty is that every child is susceptible to disconnection and the emotional struggles that accompany it. The most common cause of disconnection is passive neglect of all things authentic. Other pressures are more active and systematic in their role of disconnection. In the case of trauma, it can be immediate and profound.

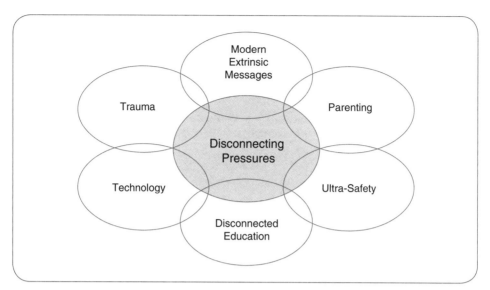

Awareness of the major players of modern-day disconnections and a Connected Classroom game plan make it possible to fight back—and win!

INTRINSIC AND EXTRINSIC PERSPECTIVES

When one considers anxiety rates were lower during the great depression, World War II, and the turbulent '60s, it would seem that the trend of increasing anxiety has more to do with shifts to cultural lifestyles and the way the world is perceived. One study suggests that the significant rise in anxiety relates to a shift from an intrinsic to extrinsic belief system (Twenge, Zhang, & Im, n.d.). Researchers suggest generational increases in anxiety and depression are a response to a sense of loss of control as they relate to a dependence on external reward.

Intrinsic rewards are a reflection of connections with authentic beliefs and align directly with the body's natural reward system. The behavior–reward relationship is simple. Connections with others, contribution, play, following a passion, or freely diving into challenge will always trigger a healthy and rewarding emotional response. Extrinsic rewards on the other hand are more complex, conditional, and muted by comparison. *Extrinsic goals* refer to beliefs that fall outside our most authentic wants and relate to things like grades, money, popularity, or good looks. The rewards of an extrinsic or disconnected belief system are dependent on material prizes, comparative status, and the judgment of others.

Working hard toward personal growth or learning will always be emotionally rewarding when viewed from an intrinsic perspective. However, a student working within an extrinsic belief system may fall short of any payoff at all because there is no guarantee working hard will result in a good grade, lavish praise, or a comparative rise in status. In this case, failure to receive an extrinsic reward will reduce the attractiveness of hard work and the otherwise healthy behavior.

Things become even more complex when children attempt to find authentic rewards from love, belonging, or self-worth within an extrinsic disconnected belief system. When a child believes a parent's approval or love is dependent on a grade, good behavior, or exemplary achievement, their authentic feelings of safety and belonging are in a constant state of jeopardy. They may work hard, and try to make good choices, but in comparative terms, still underachieve. It could also be possible that the subjective marking of a teacher is off on any particular day. Either way, the loss of control and conditionality may result in the triggering of an anxious survival mode response.

There is a sense of control when a person's behaviors or experiences follow their true-self beliefs. Connected people know what matters to them and have little difficulty making choices that govern their emotions and fate, regardless of their circumstance. Authentic feelings are hard to steal because they come from within and remain a reliable constant. Disconnected people, on the other hand, are victim to experiences and cultural pressures that tell them what to do, how to think, and who to be. Most fall short of imposed standards, but even the winners experience muted rewards. Only authentic targets beget authentic payoffs. It is comforting to know what they are.

This gets to the crux of why connectedness is so important for children. They have little control over the extrinsic world thrust on them. At school, they seek authentic reward, but finding authentic targets can be a challenge in a system driven by grades and approval by others. Shooting at extrinsic targets will always result in an authentic miss. Children become a victim of false circumstance, and anxiety rises with a loss of control over their lives. They desperately seek feelings of love, belonging, and authentic purpose in all the wrong places.

MODERN MESSAGES, PARENTING, AND CHILDREN'S AUTHENTIC TRUTH

Children live in a world bombarded by messages telling them to be something they are not. The immediate blame tends to go to advertisers, social media, and the entertainment industry. Their presence is certainly pervasive and influential, but disconnection starts closer to home. Children watch their parents' lives caught up in the pursuit of prestigious careers, pricey homes, and consumer excess. Parents scrutinizing their own behavior see the hypocrisy, but it is hard to avoid the pervasive expectations of our culture. Children see the time and effort put into these less authentic pursuits, and there is a legitimized assumption that extrinsic goals and reward are indeed the most important things in life.

The true self of a child becomes apparent early in life to parents looking for it. Typically, they can proudly use a single word to describe the prevailing attributes of their youngster. Johnny is a little athlete, and Jenny is a talented artist. Parents want the best for their child and are motivated to help them develop and grow into the best version of what they think their child could become. This is where further confusion or disconnection from a child's true self may begin. What parent does not secretly hope that their child rises to the top of the class, becomes a doctor, and lives a life of financial success?

There is nothing wrong with these goals, but it is unreasonable to believe this can or should be the path for every child. Although it is years in the future, parents begin worrying about their child's ability to pay for a home and garner respect in their community, so it is understandable that there may be a little push in a direction that may not be aligned with the authentic passions or essence of their child.

A child's authentic wants being ignored or trumped by the beliefs and expectations of their parents poses a potentially dangerous situation. A child could easily interpret the confusing scenario as a form of conditional love. Love and approval are basic needs of a child so they will attempt to align their lives with less authentic beliefs, even if it means sacrificing their true self. This may be the beginning of conditioning to seek approval from others rather than celebrating the gifts they have to share. Their sense of self is no longer good enough, and an insecure and anxious child emerges. Acting out to get the attention or approval they need becomes a reasonable coping strategy.

Parents want the best for their children. They often believe more schooling, more homework, or more structured cultural or sport programs will push them in a good direction. Inevitably, the developmental advantages of play, childlike passion, and fantasy get lost in the crunch for time. Meaningful play, passionate endeavors, creativity, and critical thought take time. Hunter-gatherer children had virtually all day to develop social skills, test limits, solve problems, and learn in a self-directed way. Limitless time for play and natural development has been replaced by rushed, scheduled lifestyles that fall short of the healthy attachment mark.

Connections with authentic truth and passion are always a good thing whether they fit in with society's ideals or not. They are not right or wrong. Adults may inadvertently stifle the power of passion when dismissing the silly dreams of young children as unimportant. I want to be a pro hockey player, skater, dancer, astronaut, archaeologist, or rock star. An authentic passion is valuable regardless of what it is, because a passion pursued is an authentically rewarding experience.

When children are encouraged to follow and experience their passions, a benchmark for what authentic reward feels like is established. Assuming it is a positive experience, they will wish to carry those pleasurable feelings into other aspects of their life. Ones that perhaps, their parents feel are more practical. If the passion is authentic and healthy, be grateful it exists, hang on to it, and help children run with it. Regardless of the superficial relevance to lifelong goals, passionate childhood experiences nurture healthy neural networks making it easier to feel in passionate ways throughout their life.

Anxiety Pro-Tip for Parents

Anxiety, Anxiety, Anxiety .... It is on every parent's radar, and talking about anxiety with children can often take on a life of its own. Thinking about it excessively can become an obsession for children that may add to or exacerbate the problem. Instead of managing anxiety through talk and cognitive coaching, put energy into creating real connected experiences that reduce stress and nurture lasting healthy neural connections and attachments. The best way to let go of unhealthy emotions is to replace them with healthy ones.

ULTRA-SAFETY

Risk plays a fundamental role in stretching the boundaries of what children already know, do, and feel. Moderate amounts of anxiety, fear, or stress are normal during challenge and learning. Exposure to these feelings plays a critical role in the development of resiliency attachments and healthy coping strategies. Ultra-safe environments limiting exposure to challenge and stressful feelings may directly create a far more dangerous scenario: an inability to cope with even mild failure or trauma.

Without challenge, risk, or fear the opportunity to be brave and grow does not exist!

The authentic drive to provide safety for children rarely seems to leave the minds of parents regardless of how busy they become. Providing a safe environment is one of the most important roles of the parent. When the perception of danger feels near, it certainly comes first in order of sequential priority. Providing safety is a benchmark for which all parents judge themselves, and in some cases, it is a focal point of judgment by others.

In a similar way, every teacher has felt, or will feel, the wrath of an overprotective parent or litigious society. There is considerable cultural pressure to provide an ultra-safe environment in a society perceived as dangerous. The freedom once enjoyed by children to go outside, take risk, play, and discover with their friends, without adult supervision, is frowned upon.

Efforts to build self-esteem in children are often confused with absolute safety and a never fail agenda. It is a difficult thing for any parent to watch a child fail or struggle, but it is unclear why many have become so hypersensitive in this regard. The cynic might suggest parents simply dislike this difficult and uncomfortable part of child-rearing, but an honest perspective also suggests the challenge is greater than it once was because parents themselves have grown up in a society that does not equate failure or struggle with growth and learning. On almost all levels, our culture and educational system classifies and divides children by their failures and struggles in a negative way. Parents fear this and want to protect their children from that. Even young children are intuitive enough to notice inauthentic celebrations over meaningless or unchallenging tasks designed to stack the deck against task-oriented failure. If my parents are protecting me from failure, it must be truly terrifying and dangerous.

One day, it is assumed, children will be out on their own and responsible for their own safety. Few things are more hazardous than a young adult lacking resiliency and the necessary coping skills to manage challenge or a truly dangerous scenario. The anxious survival responses and panic that follows only increase the danger. The best-case situation is when children have learned the skills and confidence to cope with challenge rather than simply avoiding it. In real life, avoidance or hiding is not always an option.

 TRY THIS!

Go Climb a Fence!

Teach children how to climb a fence: The lesson is about feelings of safety, support, and healthy attachments:

- Teach specific techniques of climbing.

- Learn to spot for safety.

- Use supportive language.

- Recognize anxiety in others.

- Reinforce resiliency with healthy thought patterns that reduce fear.

- Celebrate the role of helping others.

Note that climbing the fence is a task but not the objective. The underlying point of the lesson is to build resiliency through challenge and healthy coping attachments. Effective peer coaching skills tip the scales in favor of healthy attachments and the homeostatic drive. Knowing that the lesson is about support, safety, and overcoming fear grounds the emotions of students with a sense of security. There is no surprise. A moderately anxious challenge is coming, but things will be okay! Your friends have your back.

Learning the skills of support and celebrating one's role in helping others is a lesson that can be used time and time again in any challenging lesson. For some children climbing a fence will trigger significant anxiety, for others it may be a class presentation or reading out loud to others. Practicing peer support skills is a rewarding and a powerful tool in reducing fear and anxiety.

A DISCONNECTED EDUCATION

Schooling has evolved to become the main vehicle for cultural transmission, meeting societal needs, and to a certain degree, obedience. In a disconnected society, it is reasonable to suggest the education experience is by default, a systematic engine for disconnection. Young children enter the school system with their own interests and a voracious drive to freely explore and discover the world around them. They celebrate their efforts with unbridled excitement, but often discover their interests, choices, and measurements of their own successes no longer matter. As the year's pass, testing and grades become the predominant driver of learning and measurement of their success. In this respect, a child's education may systematically force him toward extrinsic reward and unhealthy emotional attachments. Perhaps to their developmental detriment, structured schooling is beginning at even earlier ages in the race to get ahead in the educational rat race.

Just about every aspect of the educational experience is out of students' control. They could be trapped with an uncaring teacher or have to endure the daily abuse of a bully who sits nearby. Choosing to avoid the pervasive competition in the classroom and the hallways is almost impossible. An extrinsically driven educational experience that only celebrates the champions means that most students will never meet the standards. It is almost the perfect recipe for a disconnecting experience.

CULTURAL DISCONNECTIONS IN EDUCATION

A disconnected education also closely parallels the achievement gap experienced by students of color or minority groups. Some people suggest a "culture of poverty" or culturally weak ties toward the value of education are to blame. Access to quality schools and teachers is categorically problematic. Inexperienced teachers or teachers deemed *less effective* are often placed at underfunded urban schools at the same time that highly effective teachers are rewarded with positions at high-performing schools (Education Trust, 2006). Other studies suggest disadvantaged students are often subject to less challenging, repetitive, rote-learning teaching models (Allington& McGill-Franzen, 1989). They routinely receive less instruction of the higher-order skill sets they need to become independent learners. Students need this type of productive struggle for healthy brain development (Means& Knapp, 1991). As students fall behind and designations like *slow learner* emerge, frustration and shame inevitably lead to a survival response and off-task defiant behavior. In turn, teachers set low expectations that further hamper growth.

In her book, *Culturally Responsive Teaching and the Brain*, Zaretta Hammond (2015) responds to these challenges with a unique perspective. She describes culture as software for the brain's hardware. The brain uses cultural information to make sense of everyday happenings and events (Hammond, 2015). She suggests this is where a disconnecting disadvantage occurs. European and North American cultures filter experiences through an individual mindset that values achievement, competition, and independence. African, Latino, and First Nation cultures tend to lean strongly toward collective perspectives that embrace relationships, community, and cooperative learning (Hofstede, Hofstede, & Minkov, 2010). Ironically, the healthy connected learning perspectives discussed in this book are largely denied to the cultures that depend on them and value them the most.

Many of these same cultures have relied on the spoken word rather than written to share knowledge and preserve traditions. Cultural experiences at home have nurtured neural networking patterns that support communication and learning through story, songs, dance, alliteration, and emotional expressions. Another disconnect and disadvantage emerges in existing school structures dependent on written-based learning that requires little personal interaction or dialogue. Their brains are wired one way, but they are asked to learn in another. A way that is arguably unnatural and unhealthy. These students are not broken or deficient. In a sense, we are expecting them to learn in another language and still win at a game they are not meant to play.

> *"Culturally responsive teachers take advantage of the fact that our brains are wired for connection."*
> —Zarreta Hammond (2015)

Numerous studies have demonstrated that culturally responsive education can strengthen student connectedness with school and enhance learning (Kalyanpur & Harry, 2012). In the chart below, Hammond (2015) outlines some of her key practice areas for teachers wishing to be culturally responsive.

READY FOR RIGOR FRAMEWORK

Awareness

- Acknowledge their own sociopolitical position
- Sharpen their cultural lens
- Manage their socio-emotional response to student diversity

Learning Partnerships

- Nurture authentic connections of trust and respect
- Use these connections to challenge students and hold them to high standards

Community Building

- Integrate universal cultural elements into the classroom
- Use cultural practices and orientations to create a safe place

Information Processing

- Understand how culture influences brain processing
- Align the learning experience in culturally congruent ways

 TRY THIS!

Set a Culturally Responsive Intention

Curricular Intention: Take your pick of topics from math, science, English, or physical education. Bring content to life in a culturally responsive way.

Connection Intention: Learn in culturally responsive ways—Teach a content lesson in a manner that reflects the learning styles of different cultures. This may include storytelling, songs, drumming, dance, art, or learning through doing. This intention is not an informative lesson about different cultures. It focuses on acknowledging, respecting, and celebrating how other cultures learn.

DISCONNECTION AND MEDIA TECHNOLOGY

Gatherings of smug over-40-year-old crowds often reminisce about the good old days when parents opened the door in the morning and children gleefully ran out to join friends at the park. They rode bikes, climbed trees, and played kick-the-can. Imagination was king, and forts became castles. They fell down, got dirty, laughed, and kept playing until it was time to go home. Yet most would have to admit the experience wasn't quite that idyllic and romantic. Their own parents proclaimed that television was already tearing the connected family lifestyle apart. Atari and

PAC-MAN became the latest craze cutting into time set aside for natural play, valued chores, and family sharing. Despite varied generational perceptions of cultural shifts, the influences of new media technologies have been pedestrian when compared to the rapid all-consuming changes to come.

Ironically, parents may share a significant role in stifling the authentic face-to-face experiences they remember as valuable in their own youth. A point often missed concerning complaints about overuse of social media technology is that modern children and teens are no different from their parents in their youth. A natural need to connect with their peers drives their behavior. "Keep them busy and they will stay out of trouble." Sport, tutorials, and cultural activities become the perceived safer alternative and quickly fill the daily agenda. Add in the time demands of homework, and what choice does a teenager have but to turn on a convenient device? The constraints of their superbusy schedules may make media technology the only practical option to connect with their peers in an unstructured way.

THINK ABOUT IT

Unhealthy Daily Numbers

- The average number of texts for teens is 118.

- 18% text over 200 times.

- The average elementary student spent 5.5 hours engaged in some form of media technology (Rideout, Foehr, & Roberts, 2010).

For some children, texts and tweets become the lone skill set for peer communication. Authentic face-to-face connections become an anxious experience because it requires far more intuitive and complex communication abilities they may lack. Online social media users have time to ponder that perfect witty response, and there is no need to put energy into reading body language or voice tone. If the conversation is uncomfortable, resolution isn't necessary because the option exists to move on to hundreds of other online friends.

Social media has become the primary source of communication and interaction among youth outside of school. Sadly, kindness, contribution, and joyful exchanges are not always part of the process. Cyber bullying and online predators plague the headlines and add to the anxiety of both children and parents. Electronic media exposes children to unhealthy visuals that may create a perverse version of what fitting in means. For many, popularity and self-value have become a function of the number of tweets, texts, and Facebook friends a child makes, none of which translate into natural, authentic emotional payoffs.

It is unquestionable that technology is here to stay and will likely become only more pervasive in our culture so a practical perspective on healthy use is necessary. We live in the technological age, and denying the important role it will play in the future education, careers, and social lives of children is dishonest. It is a vital component for access to knowledge, and mastery of it is required for a competitive edge in the information age. Technology is not good or bad; it is just a tool, and using it in healthy ways depends on how or, more important, why we use it.

Advocates of social media technology argue its use is better than no connection at all and, if used intelligibly, could lead to more face-to-face connection. However, for those who lose themselves in their devices and are unable to make the transition to natural exchanges, the situation changes somewhat. If time commitments to technology are such that they are impeding opportunities or the desire for necessary healthy activities, then addiction needs to be considered as part of the discussion.

TRY THIS!

To avoid almost certain pushback in response to external control over technology use, children and teens need to be involved with creating consistent structure and viable alternatives. An honest and open dialogue about the risks, pitfalls, and benefits of technology is an excellent way to give ownership to students over usage. Embracing their ideas for using technology in healthy ways is an excellent strategy for buy in.

It is becoming more challenging to dismiss the negative effects of technology addiction. A review of psychological literature of online social networking and addiction suggests that excessive use of social networking may be particularly addictive to young people (Kuss & Griffiths, 2011). They discuss studies that claim symptoms of social networking addictions are similar to those of substance or behavior addictions like gambling. Children who overuse technology appear to experience physiological changes that mimic those seen in high stress states, such as high heart rates, fast-paced breathing, and hyperacute hearing and vision (Rowan, 2010). Not surprisingly, they are describing symptoms that mimic survival mode.

Concerned voices are getting louder as parents and teachers alike take note of rising health and developmental issues, social dysfunction, and declining academic performance. Studies draw links between technology overuse and a delay in children's achievement of sensory and motor milestones (Rowan, 2010), and exposure to violent content during gaming has been correlated with aggression and reduced empathy (Gentile & Bushman, 2012). Technology addiction is a real thing, and it is putting more and more students at a disadvantage in the classroom.

TECHNOLOGY ADDICTIONS IN THE CLASSROOM

Smart phones with social media and gaming apps in the pockets of students can be a serious distraction to learning and authentic connections in the classroom. Teachers can easily become stuck in repetitive battles with students over usage during lessons. Loose or inconsistent structure can result in a perpetual state of distraction when children anxiously wonder if it is okay to use devices so they end up thinking about being online more than do those guided by firm structure. Drama attached to control usage invariably amplifies emotional imbalance and inhibits focused engaged learning.

TRY THIS!

When smart phones chronically distract from authentic learning, have students check in their phones at the start of class. Routine quickly becomes the norm. Smart phones are a valuable learning tool. If a student needs it for a specific task, it is easily accessible if the use is justified.

TRAUMA AND THE RISE OF THE FALSE-SELF PERSONA

Anxiety, stress, and emotional pain are not the problem. The inability to let it go is. The benchmark for positive stress is that it goes away when it is no longer necessary. The benchmark for trauma is stress frozen in place, locked by unhealthy neural attachments and chemical imbalance. Any trauma is a terrible thing, but how a child responds to the trauma is far more important than its perceived severity.

Sometimes bad things happen. Accidents, the loss of a loved one, illness, and criminal assault are traumatic experiences that may trigger survival mode in even the most balanced individual. Trauma can also be the result of natural disasters, social upheaval, or poverty. Discrimination by race, gender, or religious beliefs can trigger intense feelings of fear, shame, or anger. Whether the experience is lived or simply seen in the media does not matter, it can be traumatic and a direct threat to feelings of communal and personal safety. Children are the most vulnerable to these traumas because their brains freely respond and adapt to the emotional experience. They are in a precarious position if they lack the resiliency attachments they need for emotional recovery.

It is because of these vulnerabilities that trauma does not have to be headline news to cause life-altering adaptations to a child's brain. Perceived abuse, neglect, parental divorce, or family dysfunction potentiates a similar response. At school, bullying or constant failure may be the culprit. A survival mode response is expected and normal. However, the all-important question remains. Will it go away?

During or after trauma, people will always attach to emotions as part of their coping strategy (see Fig 4.1). Those deeply attached to their true self have the ability to stay connected with the core beliefs and healthy emotions that carry them through difficult times or experiences. A healthy connected and supported individual is more resilient if she believes in the love, stability, and safety of her world beyond the trauma. For those lacking authentic connections, trauma can become a perpetual catastrophic experience of unending emotional pain. If the emotions of the trauma are overwhelming to the point that authentic connections and the homeostatic drive are too weak to pull a person out of survival mode, the painful emotion experienced during the trauma continues to linger and take hold in the form of unhealthy neural attachments.

FIGURE 4.1

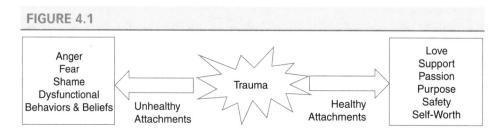

When a person is unable to let go of these painful emotions, coping strategies evolve to include unhealthy behaviors that inevitably lead to more drama and pain. Attachments to these behaviors come with unhealthy thought patterns, beliefs, and stories causing a person to relive the specific emotions of the trauma in an addictive loop of unending survival states and emotional imbalance. This profound disconnection may give rise to an unhealthy false-self persona where these attachments form a new identity dominating a child's life and unjustly defining who he is (Montgomery, 2010). Johnny is angry, fearful, or insecure. Compensatory dysfunctional behaviors hide true-self identities, leaving the disconnected judged, and condemned. Johnny is rude, disruptive, and a bully. His false-self identity is reinforced and disconnection from those he loves and the things that matter most deepens.

Youth become gang members, drug users, cutters, or followers of questionable alternative groups because they are desperate for any lifeline of safety or control in their life of perpetual chaos. No child dreams of one day flipping the finger at the world with an "I don't care" identity. No person would consciously choose an identity that most certainly makes life worse. Yet, for some reason, they do. This is the nature of all addiction. It buries authentic truth in stories of false-self lies that are difficult to let go.

DISCONNECTING PRESSURES AND EMOTIONAL ADDICTION

All disconnecting pressures, whether they are related to media culture, overprotective parents, a competitive educational experience, or very real painful trauma, are interpreted by our hunter-gatherer physiology as a survival threat. The deck is stacked against children, but they do not have to be helpless victims of perpetual emotional pain. The next chapter delves deeper into the workings of emotional addiction and the mechanics of how it maliciously incites emotional pain and reinforces the story that tells a child she is something other than who she truly is. Teachers who know the game will know how to win it.

Inubu

War

The peace and safety of the settlement was a distant memory. For some time now, the insurgents had been wreaking havoc in the remote jungle territory they called home. Circumstances had forced him into a role the boy questioned if he was ready for. The young hunter knew the forest well and led the women and children to the cave that was once his refuge. He had done his job well, but now it was time to return home and join the men who had defended the village.

As he entered the settlement, his heart sank. Smoke billowed from the ruins of the smoldering grass huts. Blackened bloody bodies were scattered among the chaos. The smell of burning flesh sickened him as it filled his nostrils, but he could think of nothing more than finding his father. Rage and anguish propelled him through the wreckage in his desperate search. The first body was unrecognizable if not for the familiar necklace of his beloved uncle. He paused to process the shocking sight. Breathing was difficult. His hand covered his mouth in an effort not to vomit.

"Inubu."

It was a weak voice, but it was enough to fill him with hope as he scrambled to his father's side. It was bad. Very bad.

His father was powerful and strong, but his wounds were severe. Inubu shook with his own emotional pain that radiated throughout his body. He could only imagine the agony the brave man was enduring, yet somehow a smile spread across his father's face. He was pleased that his son was safe. His hand squeezed Inubu's own with the little strength he had. He took a shallow breath.

"The world is good."

"Think love." … "And share love."

With that, his father's chest rose and fell for the last time.

CHAPTER 5

Addiction in the Classroom

Students have already had the "don't drink or do drugs" lecture, and this chapter is not another version of the same. It is about recognizing repetitive, destructive patterns of behavior and beliefs that cycle students through emotional highs and lows, knocking their lives out of balance. Sadly, alcohol and substance abuse do exist in schools. In this discussion, however, those terms are only a reference point to understanding a broader definition of addiction—one that is more relevant in the classroom.

Sometimes behaviors in the classroom do not follow reason. The hyperactive student bouncing about in her seat endures constant scorn from the teacher frustrated by interruptions. A bully continuously sent to the office experiences the same isolation that may have triggered his anger in the first place. Another student is distracted as she impatiently awaits the next insignificant text. Drama erupts as the teacher takes her phone away yet again. None of these behaviors make the life of a student better. In fact, they chronically and senselessly draw the student toward a deepening state of emotional pain. This is the nature of the addictive drive.

WHY DO CHILDREN BEHAVE AND THINK THE WAY THEY DO?

The answer to this question is not as complicated as one might think because the answer is almost always the same. They act and think in certain ways in the pursuit of emotional reward. In a perfect world, children would be driven by authentic rewards that make life better, but this is not always the case. The addictive drive is deceptive and comes with its own very powerful emotional rewards. The addictive and homeostatic drives compete for supremacy and influence in the lives of our students (see Figure 5.1).

FIGURE 5.1

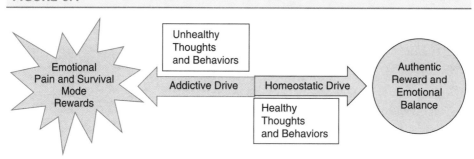

ADDICTION

The term *addiction* has negative connotations of weakness and dependency. Some teachers might struggle using the term in fear of labeling children as addicts and excusing unacceptable behavior. The exact opposite is more the reality. Addiction is not an inescapable condition that defines an individual in a truthful way. When an honest understanding of what drives dysfunctional behavior is exposed, knowledge and awareness replace excuses. If the true-self story is powerful enough to become believable, even the most serious biochemical addiction becomes a choice.

To recognize the wide spectrum of addiction, it is necessary to let go of the fears associated with the term. All addiction is identified by chronic belief or behavior that inevitably ends in ever-increasing unnecessary pain and dysfunction. To some degree, addictive tendencies are part of every person's life. We all have a weak spot for beliefs or behaviors that ultimately make life worse. Accepting this for what it is creates the awareness needed to stay balanced in the most connected way possible.

For many years experts believed only alcohol and drugs could cause addiction, but recent research has shown activities such as gambling, sex, or compulsive shopping could also cause similar corruptions to neural pathways related to pleasure and desire. Addiction corrupts the reward centers of the brain by changing the way we experience pleasure. It then corrupts other drives such as learning (habit) and motivation (wanting) (Shaffer, 2017).

Advances in neuroscience have revealed many breakthroughs in how addiction works, but even the experts agree many questions remain. The addiction mechanisms discussed in this book are not meant to be definitive explanations for how addiction works. The intention is to create a working way to think about the neurological link between addiction, disconnection, the survival response, and the way emotional reward is processed (see Figure 5.2). A working understanding will help teachers plan lessons to reduce the stress response and chronic unhealthy emotions linked to the addictive drive.

FIGURE 5.2

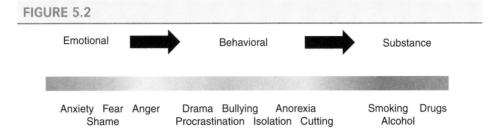

| Emotional | → | Behavioral | → | Substance |

| Anxiety Fear Anger
Shame | Drama Bullying Anorexia
Procrastination Isolation Cutting | Smoking Drugs
Alcohol |

Smoking, drugs, or dangerous, compulsive behaviors are never a first addiction. The commonality among all these beliefs and behaviors is disconnection, trauma, and unhealthy, emotional attachments.

SOURCE: Montgomery & Ritchey, 2010

DISCONNECTION AND ADDICTION

Renowned addiction expert Gabor Mate (2012) strongly suggests that childhood trauma or disconnection rather than choice, chance, or genetic predetermination determines a person's susceptibility to addiction. Humans and animals require nurturing to survive, and when insufficient connected experiences or exposures to excessively stressful ones occur, marked alterations to neurotransmitter and reward systems dramatically increase the likelihood of addiction. He suggests the lingering stress response results in hormone levels that disrupt the emotional and reward centers of the brain. Stress, real or imagined, disturbs homeostasis, and he concludes in general that it is a serious precursor for addiction (Mate, 2012).

> "It may be said without hesitation that for man the most important stressors are emotional."
>
> —Gabor Mate (2012)

Studies have shown college students with the least healthy parent relationships often experience a dramatic stress response when giving public speeches or taking stressful tests. In some cases, the stress levels become so high that cortisol and dopamine levels released compare to the effects of methamphetamines. Students with stronger loving parental attachments show levels of cortisol and dopamine as much as two to three times lower under similar circumstances (Pruessner, Champagne, Meaney, & Dagher, 2004).

It might be hard to compare the survival response and payoff generated by chronic anxiety over daily quizzes to the intense reward of a narcotic like cocaine, but the underlying mechanism is similar and the addiction to both may be challenging for the same reasons. While the damaging effects of emotional addiction may seem less significant, they should not be underestimated. In the case of phobias or panic attacks, the addictive biochemical payoffs are potentially far greater than that of many narcotics.

Comparing one type of addiction to another in terms of relative perceived severity may be misleading. The more damaging aspect of emotional addiction is the staggering numbers of children suffering from chronic anxiety, fear, shame, or anger. This makes it a far greater problem in schools than drugs or alcohol. Regardless of where it falls on the spectrum, all addiction begins with an attachment to unhealthy emotions during or after trauma. These attachments represent the simplest type of addiction where children are trapped in an addictive cycle of rewards derived from stress hormones associated with painful emotions (Montgomery & Ritchey, 2008). Emotional drama is all a person needs for the next addictive high.

THE WHY AND HOW OF FEELINGS, EMOTIONS, AND ADDICTION

"Jaak Panksepp was an Estonian-American neuroscientist and psychobiologist who coined the term 'affective neuroscience,' the name for the field that studies the neural mechanisms of emotion" (Panksepp, n.d.). When discussing why we have emotions, his answer was simple and succinct:

> *"We have feelings because they tell us what supports survival or detracts from our survival."*
> *(Panksepp, 2014)*

In other words, feelings like love drive us toward connections with others. Lust drives us to reproduce. Fear is a survival response and encourages us to avoid a danger. This all makes perfect sense as a survival strategy. In a healthy, balanced brain, the system should work quite effectively.

How addiction happens is neuroscience. It occurs when adaptations trick our brain into believing we need more of something to survive. More specifically, neurological shifts create conditions that tell the brain a survival response makes sense when no danger really exists. The adaptation throws the brain out of balance and creates the chronic emotional highs and lows that define addiction.

THE CHEMISTRY OF EMOTIONAL ADDICTION

Several studies have shown dopamine and endorphins play significant roles in drug addiction (Robinson & Berridge, 2016). Dopamine is a neurotransmitter generally accepted as the primary driver of the wanting or desire element of addiction. New evidence suggests that endorphins also play a role in the process by providing a feeling of pleasure or reducing pain (Montgomery & Ritchy, 2008).

In 1972, researchers Candace Pert and Solomon Snyder (1973) at John Hopkins University discovered the human brain had specific receptor sites for opiate drugs like heroin, codeine, and morphine. At first, they were puzzled why these sites existed, but they soon surmised that the active ingredient in all these opiates had a very similar structure to naturally occurring endorphins.

Endorphins are feel-good chemicals produced in the reward centers of the brain allowing people to experience pleasure in response to connected experiences like sex, exercise, food, or touch. Surprisingly, the release of endorphins also occurs from the same area of the brain when people are stressed or in pain. Survival mode responses trigger a flood of endorphins creating an analgesic effect to ease potential pain in a manner similar to that of opiates like heroin, codeine, or morphine. This is why endorphins are often called the *natural opiates* of the body.

Many addictive drugs rely on a massive stressful survival response to achieve their effect (Montgomery & Ritchey, 2008). In the case of emotional trauma or chronic disconnection, when stress levels remain abnormally high, neural adaptations occur in a similar way to that of chronic drug use as the brain attempts to manage the overloading flood of dopamine and endorphins related to the survival response.

Fight, flight, or freeze emotions are necessary, but temporary, responses to cope with trauma or survival threats. In times of danger, they make sense, because the elevated response helps cope with a threatening scenario. Letting go of emotions like anger or fear when danger recedes is an important part of returning to a balanced homeostatic state. Emotions that linger beyond the trauma are no longer necessary and may be indicative of unhealthy emotional attachments that keep potentially damaging stress hormone levels high. The addictive drive is ready to take advantage of any obsession with negative emotions.

Survival mode emotions are the fuel for addiction. Irrational feelings are cheap, easy, and readily accessible for a child without an authentic payoff option. Reliving emotions of past traumas can generate multiple endorphin payoffs. People with chronic depression have demonstrated a significant endorphin release when simply asked to think of emotionally painful thoughts (Kennedy, Koeppe, Young, & Zubieta, 2006). Creating an overly dramatic replay from something as simple as classroom failure, an embarrassing moment among peers, or a fight with their parents can turn up the volume on the emotional state. What could possibly be the reason for obsessing over emotionally painful stories from the past?

Moving past emotional experiences means sacrificing the unhealthy payoffs of the addictive drive. If healthy authentic rewards are not a viable option, there really is no choice but to unconsciously hang onto or incite unnecessary painful emotions for continued payoffs. Unhealthy payoffs come with the illusion that they are better than no payoff at all because they give a temporary reprieve and sense of control, even if they inevitably cause deepening disconnection from life's authentic joys.

> *"Children with video game addictions are generally those for whom other authentically satisfying forms of play have not been available."*
> (Przybyski, Weinstein, Ryan, & Rigby, 2009)

The Highs and Lows of Unnecessary Emotional Pain

Brain imaging studies have shown that emotionally painful experiences activate many of the same areas of the brain activated by physical pain (Eisenberger & Lieberman, 2004). Furthermore, endorphins released as part of the stress response dull both emotional and physical pain (Volpicelli, Balaraman, Hahn, Wallace, & Bux, 1999). This suggests the human brain does not differentiate between the unnecessary emotional pain of dramatic false-self stories and the physical pain that may accompany trauma. It does not matter if the trauma is real or imagined. The response is real, and the chemistry works the same.

The endorphin payoffs that accompany emotional drama are significant and are a worthy opponent for the healthy endorphin payoffs of homeostatic drive. The repetitive cycle of emotional addiction works in similar ways. As a result, the brain begins to show adaptation and a change of circuitry in the same way that it does for opiates. Tolerance to the massive endorphin payoffs becomes a factor as the body attempts to oppose the high of the swing and bring chemical levels to a more balanced equilibrium. Eventually the analgesic effects of endorphins diminish. High levels of dopamine during the stress response complicate matters. The intense wanting dopamine creates increases at the same time the pleasurable effects of endorphins diminish (Berridge & Robinson, 2016). The irrational nature and attractiveness of emotional addiction starts to make more sense.

In this scenario, even greater levels of endorphins are necessary to achieve the same high. This means that emotional drama and dysfunction will have to up their game. This is what may drive children to behaviors considered more dangerous on the addiction spectrum. Regardless of the addiction they pursue, there will always be the need for greater payoffs unless the cycle is broken.

Another commonality between the self-destructive patterns of all addictions is the crash after the temporary high. As endorphin levels plummet below normal levels in a rebound effect, a person suffering from addiction experiences a significant chemical imbalance and feelings of depression. Feelings of hopelessness, fatigue, and physical sickness, not unlike conditions of withdrawal experienced by the alcoholic or drug abuser, characterize the crash. The extreme lows are uncomfortable and create a powerful desire for the next high. This is the beginning of dependence on the next emotional fix. Desperate behaviors begin to make sense. If simple "poor me," anger, shame, or "less than" addictions cannot generate sufficient payoffs, it may be time to move on to other unhealthy behaviors on the addiction spectrum.

An unfair fight?

The payoffs of the addictive drive swing back and forth in a perpetual state of imbalance and constant unhealthy payoffs. *There is no crash with an authentic payoff* (see Figure 5.3), and therefore no desperate drive for the next fix.

FIGURE 5.3

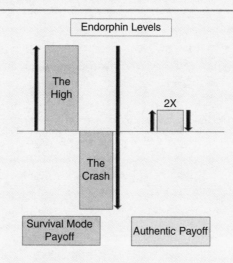

BEHAVIOR ADDICTIONS

If reliving emotions of past trauma does not meet the needs of an out-of-balance child, payoffs derived from dysfunctional behaviors are an excellent way to rekindle survival states for potentially greater payoffs. Creating emotional pain requires little imagination. Unhealthy behaviors breeding drama between classmates, the teacher, or even within themselves can easily wind up unhealthy emotions. Children unconsciously driven toward survival mode payoffs chronically break rules, disturb others, and seek ways to hurt themselves emotionally. When the behavior is physically destructive, as in the case of cutting, emotional pain remains the true target that promises to deliver the reward they unconsciously seek.

Addiction will drive students to behave poorly in an unconscious way, not for the thrill of the act itself, but for the emotional payoff of the oncoming punishment, conflict, or drama. This is an important distinction for a teacher to understand, because taking the behavior head-on with management, control, or discipline may be exactly what the addiction wants.

Chronic procrastination is an excellent example of a passive-aggressive strategy to invoke a perpetual out-of-balance emotional state. An anxious obsession over the impending conflict for avoiding a relatively meaningless task will receive a constant flow of unhealthy biochemical reward. Procrastination is bait for a larger conflict. The harder a teacher or parent tries to control the behavior, the greater the conflict, drama, and, ultimately, payoff. Addictive behaviors love strict rules, a heavy hand, and threatening control because stepping over the line potentiates the greatest drama. Simple but chronic behaviors like talking loudly, bouncing in a chair, or off-task behaviors could be an unconscious attempt to trigger an emotionally charged conflict with a teacher.

In other cases, the drama becomes a more passive, internal conflict where the student withdraws to the pain of a "poor me" attachment in response to discipline or their behavior being shut down. Controlling behavior is only a superficial win for the teacher even if it brings temporary order to the classroom. A child remains in emotional pain. It is only a matter of time until their chronic anxiety causes serious health issues or addiction elevates its game to cause greater distress and disconnection.

The hormone swings of the addictive drive and chronic stress play havoc with the health of children. Rising cortisol levels adversely affect immune systems and sugar levels. Dopamine levels that are too high or too low impair memory and attention. Symptoms of low endorphin levels include nausea and excessive sensitivity to emotional or physical pain (see Figure 5.4). It is little wonder the chronically disconnected struggle at school. That is, of course, if they come at all.

FIGURE 5.4

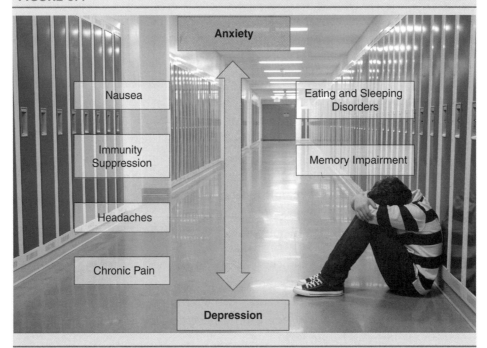

IMAGE SOURCE: iStock.com/straycat

THE EMOTIONALLY CONNECTED CLASSROOM

IS ADDICTION THE DRIVER OF ALL BAD BEHAVIOR?

Addiction is not the culprit behind most negative behaviors in the classroom. Sometimes children act inappropriately simply because they expect it might be fun, while other times it is just habit or a misguided decision. Disconnected children lack a well-defined internal compass and are more likely to engage in unhealthy behaviors, but even relatively connected children will still make poor decisions due to inexperience and an authentic drive to test boundaries.

It is part of the learning process for children to make poor choices as they explore the world, and sometimes those choices will end up buried in unpleasant emotions. A child insults a peer in a misguided attempt to be funny and hurts the feelings of her classmate. She feels regret or considers the threat of punishment or reprisal a rational deterrent. In a balanced child, those negative feelings and outcomes should be enough to dissuade him from repeating the unhealthy behavior. He apologizes, lets go of the emotions, and moves on a little wiser. A valuable lesson is learned.

In the case of the chronic bully or procrastinator, the outcome is different. The fight or flight strategy she uses to create illusionary feelings of safety results in a temporary high that is followed by an emotional crash of self-loathing, guilt, or depression. The impending isolation and punishment pushes the procrastinator or bully further behind. Her life has actually gotten worse. It is time to lash out again or care even less. There is no lesson or resolution. This outcome reinforces the unhealthy attachment that drives her behavior.

It can become confusing trying to differentiate between natural healthy mistakes or inexperience and destructive addictive behaviors, but it is a very important distinction because it determines the way a teacher responds. Mistakes are easy to address. Teachers can help students dial in on and process their natural feelings of regret and create strategies to modify or avoid the behavior in the future.

Avoiding or controlling unhealthy behaviors is not a strategy for fighting addiction. It does not change the underlying condition. Finding balance is not as simple as sidestepping or managing behaviors that we normally associate with the addictive drive. The reality is that it would take little effort to switch from one bad behavior to another and perhaps discover an even greater payoff. Even if it were hypothetically possible to address all potential bad behaviors, addiction would find another way. Addiction is incredibly resourceful and adaptable. It is willing and able to turn even the healthiest behaviors into addictive fuel. Sometimes even good behavior is just an illusion painted by the addictive drive.

HEALTHY BEHAVIORS GONE BAD

Endorphins are a primary source of pleasurable feelings associated with healthy, connected behaviors. One could easily reason that working hard, embracing challenge, or helping others are behaviors that always receive their payoff from the homeostatic drive, but this is not necessarily so. The basic human need for food is an excellent example that demonstrates how one can displace a seemingly healthy behavior into the realm of the addictive drive.

Food is a necessary healthy requirement of all living beings. A shortage of food would justifiably trigger a survival response, but supply is not really a problem for most people. When we eat, endorphin payoffs are the reward for healthy behavior and we feel a sense of pleasure and satisfaction. Payoffs continue when the meal is shared with those we love. At first glance, everything about food seems to be on the homeostatic side of the equation. However, when people begin to obsess about it, things can change quite dramatically. Over eating, bulimia, and anorexia are a reflection of a healthy behavior hijacked by the addictive drive. Lies, shame, isolation, and deepening disconnection follow.

 TRY THIS!

Think about circumstances where these behaviors could fall on either side of the Addictive-Homeostatic equation (see Figure 5.5).

FIGURE 5.5

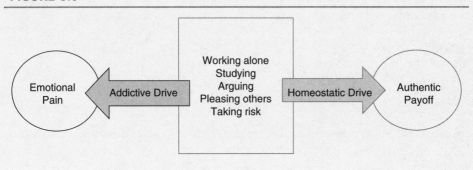

If you were able to create stories where these typical school behaviors could slide back or forth, you probably began with *the why* behind the behavior. Is the student working alone for focus and concentration on a task he believes is important or is he reinforcing the emotional pain of isolation? Teachers cannot possibly analyze every behavior that a student engages in, but they can look for patterns and emotional stories that linger in the addictive drive and chronically push students toward emotional pain.

THE EMOTIONALLY CONNECTED CLASSROOM

BELIEF ADDICTIONS AND FALSE-SELF STORIES

Attachments or addictions to unhealthy emotions usually evolve to include false-self stories that reinforce or justify those emotions long after they become unnecessary. These false-self stories express themselves as dysfunctional beliefs a child honestly accepts as true and relevant coping strategies. However, to the casual observer sharing the experience, it is obvious the belief and behavior only make the situation worse.

The child living with emotional addiction does not see things quite so clearly. She has a blind spot for rational thought when it comes to her addiction. This is because addiction is the ultimate liar. It creates dramatic, frightening stories that exist beyond reality and present moment truth. Fear, distrust, and distress infect the world of the chronically anxious child.

A quiz, an uncomfortable interaction with a peer, or an upcoming presentation hardly constitute survival situations, yet the dramatic stories and the feelings that may govern these relatively benign happenings say that they are. Addiction is a master storyteller capable of creating an unquestionable belief that the grass is blue and the sky is green. An untrue story becomes believable because their irrational feelings tell them it is.

Children attached to unhealthy false-self stories get caught up in a cycle of feelings that perpetuate the lies they accept as true. For example, a *less than* child who puts down a peer may believe their relative status has grown. The false-self or addictive drive payoff and a temporary reprieve from his emotional pain are his proof. In the short term, this reinforces the story of bullying as a meaningful strategy, but a truthful realization that his status may have actually diminished may challenge this belief. Addiction is ready for this turn of events. A new story that blames the victim or others for his emotional pain further protects the lie that justifies the behavior.

All false-self beliefs are a lie. The need to be loved, feel safe, and contribute is an undeniable truth of human nature. No child, or adult for that matter, consciously wants to exist in a disconnected state of emotional pain. Their existence is just limited to a story of negative emotions concealing their true self. Teachers trying to challenge the false-self stories of their students with rational discussion that dismisses feelings and beliefs as irrational run into a common roadblock. The high and low feelings of the addictive drive are real and undeniable. They are asking children to give up the only coping strategy and payoffs they know, and let go of what little sense of control they have in their life. Brushing aside feelings and beliefs as nonsense will undoubtedly result in pushback and escalation. The best way to get somebody to give something up is to offer something better. Give them a new story grounded in truth and authentic experience. One that gives hope.

I SEE YOU: The Opposite Game

Anxiety and the addictive drive will always create stories that attack our most authentic desires. If I am fearful, bravery will take me where I need to go. If I feel alone, I look for support that is almost certainly there. If it tells me to quit, perseverance will bring me great reward. Acknowledge anxious stories and they will always point in the opposite direction of truth. "Thank you anxiety" for telling me exactly where I need to go!

IMAGE SOURCE: Courtesy of Darryl Kimak

ALIGNMENT WITH A TRUE-SELF STORY

If addiction relies on false-self stories and lies to perpetuate itself, it stands to reason that authentic truth and experiences would be the front-line tool in the battle against it. A connected experience linking authentic emotional reward and behavior is the tangible proof that a true-self story needs to become believable and attractive. Lessons and environments aligned with authentic connections that trigger authentic payoffs and feelings tip the scales in favor of the homeostatic drive. Sometimes just imagining a vivid, hopeful, authentic experience will do the trick. Feeling is believing—and behavior will always follow belief.

Ms. Grabowski

Imagine if: An Authentic Story

Last year the CPR lesson was a disaster. What lesson could be more important than the one that might save another person's life? She presented the lesson in the step-by-step manner the manual in front of her suggested. Susan was quite wrong in assuming the boys in her class would find it interesting. It sort of was, but not in the way she hoped for as the boys were more inclined to play catch with the mannequin heads and ruthlessly pound their chests in hopes that they would magically spring back to life. They were not bad boys. Trying to save a life is a scary responsibility, and she guessed that they acted out because they were anxious about the thought of it.

She was beginning this year's lesson with one less working mannequin. Because of the fiasco, she was determined to find a way to make this year's lesson more engaging and meaningful. She sat her class down very close and began her lesson with a soft voice of concern.

"Today we are going to help each other learn how to save another human being from death. At some point in your own life, every one of you will know somebody who will suffer a heart attack. Some of you may have already experienced that tragedy. As we continue with our class today, I want you to consider that one day you could make an almost unimaginable difference. If you are prepared for that moment of need and you are brave enough to act, it may be the most important and rewarding thing you do in your entire life."

Ms. G did her best to stare into the eyes of every student before she continued.

"IMAGINE IF you are at a family gathering, laughing and enjoying a wonderful dinner when your uncle suddenly goes quiet, holds his hands to his chest, and slowly falls to the floor. Confusion erupts as your aunt scrambles to his side and hysterically calls for help as he drifts to unconsciousness. Somebody calls 911, but your aunt remains alone with her husband. Nobody steps up to act. You are afraid, but you know what to do."

Again she paused to give them time to absorb the moment and think of a loved one in their life. The students sat quietly as she continued.

"IMAGINE IF later that evening you enter the hospital room to find your aunt and cousins by your uncle's side. He was alive and doing well. On the way out the door, the paramedics told your parents that your act of bravery was the reason your uncle would probably survive. It was a proud moment but nothing compared to the emotions you feel when your aunt turns her head toward you. She says nothing as she walks toward you and embraces you in a hug. Your cousins join in with their own version of thanks as tears of gratitude begin to splash on the floor. Your uncle just smiles. You hadn't really thought about it, but you suddenly realize you saved an entire family."

The lesson went much better this year.

ONE STRATEGY FITS ALL

Teachers who understand the chemistry and nature of emotional imbalance and addiction have many distinct advantages. The first is that they recognize survival mode, even in its most subdued forms. They also recognize what fuels addiction and know how to dial down control dramas and starve the addictive drive. Isolating dysfunctional behaviors and viewing them for what they really are creates room for the compassion and patience needed for difficult times ahead. Perhaps most important of all, they enter the classroom armed with an undeniable truth of hunter-gatherer biology. All students want and need connection, even if the false-self story they live with voraciously denies it.

The human brain, physiology, and personal experiences of children are complex. A set of clean-cut answers for all the challenges children face does not exist, but a unified approach and perspective that address a majority of the dysfunctional stories and behaviors children embrace certainly simplify things. There is a powerful and hopeful upside to believing the majority of chronic dysfunction, health issues, and learning challenges in the classroom are a function of, in whole or in part, disconnection, unhealthy attachments, emotional imbalance, or addiction. It means these conditions are treatable with the most natural healing remedy available: authentic connections and experiences. Live and learn in the realm of the homeostatic drive and feed the Good Wolf. This is the path for every child, regardless of their personal challenges, to be the best and happiest version of themselves. One strategy fits all!

A New Path: Emotional Alignment

Traditional definitions of addiction are frightening and create scenarios that place meaningful influence beyond the realm of the teacher. Are teachers qualified or in a position to take on addiction? The reality is that they may be the only people who are. They have students for a large portion of the day and have great influence over their environment and daily experiences. Teachers have the power and means to create a scenario where students can feel and experience a connected life free of the disconnecting pressures of the modern world.

Emotional attachments are the building blocks for the stories and belief systems that rule our lives. Some are weak and will fade with time, while others are powerful and influence a life for years to come. They can exist as a reflection of common, everyday experiences, or they can be an expression of traumatic events. Children are who they are, for good or for bad, because of life's experiences and the emotions used to write their personal story. Fortunately, for those who have received the short end of the stick, experiences ahead can rewrite the story. One aligned with choice, healthy emotions, and the homeostatic drive.

From this perspective, classroom strategies for fighting unhealthy attachments, addiction, and chronic emotional imbalance emerge. On a daily basis, children are experiencing learning in the realm of the homeostatic drive or they are not. If they are not feeding the Good Wolf, they are feeding the Bad. Their physiology shifts toward health and emotional balance or neural dysregulation and emotional pain. If the addictive drive were a sentient entity, it would want children to feel stuck, hopeless, and embrace its lies as an inescapable fate. The homeostatic drive would want children to embrace hope, truth, and growth. It is through real daily experiences that children acquire the knowledge and inspiration to choose authentic connection as their own.

The task for teachers is clear.

Authentic attachments are always the product of authentic experiences, feel-good moments, and healthy thinking patterns. They must be lived and experienced in the biggest ways possible. The more immersive and consistent the connected experience, the more powerful the intervention becomes. The Buddhist monk simplifies his life in an effort to minimize extrinsic distraction on the journey to authentic bliss and emotional balance. Things will never be so simple at school, but learning to make all things authentic the driver of a student's education and life is an excellent start. Letting go of the importance we place on status, content, testing, and achievement eases the journey.

The next chapter takes a closer look at ways teachers can plan learning challenges that nurture connectedness and authentic, emotional attachments. Ironically, anxiety and survival mode themselves can be the vehicles that break the chains of false-self stories, unhealthy attachments, and emotional addictions. In an Emotionally Connected Classroom, it is as easy as 1-2-3.

Johnny

Survival Mode, False-Self Stories, and Unhealthy Payoffs

Johnny hated school. He wasn't smart like his brother. His reputation, for better or for worse, was all he had here. He puffed out his chest as he entered the classroom. It felt good that others were intimidated by him, but it didn't change the fact that here he felt afraid. His mind drifted back to the comfort of his game as he settled into his chair and lessons began.

The question from Ms. G startled him. He knew the answer, but in his panic a stupid response slipped out. Most kids knew better, but Stevie cracked a small smile. Johnny's blood boiled and the book flew across the room. He missed his target, but the point hit home. Ms. G didn't even have to ask. He made his way to her desk and prepared himself for, yet again, another lecture. Today he felt particularly agitated. He wasn't sure why he did it, but he looked Ms. G in the face and spit on her desk.

Her body shook with revulsion as the slime spread slowly across her desk. It had been a tough day already. Intense anger followed disbelief. She grabbed Johnny by the back of the shirt and dragged him roughly to the hallway. Susan knew it was a mistake, but at the time it didn't seem to matter. Johnny's overtly dramatic squeal of pain only enraged her more. Johnny had won this one.

He wasn't sure if he planned it that way, but this was a major victory. Something about this made him feel in control. The principal might fire her. His parents might even come to his defense. Even his classmates might feel sorry for him. He had been abused. Somebody would surely have to protect him now.

Johnny

The Crash and Hidden Truths

He had been sitting outside the principal's office for some time now. His father was on his way from work, but he was certain he wasn't coming to protect him. The rush of power he had felt earlier in the day was quickly replaced by the reality of what he had done. He cried uncontrollably. Things had actually gotten worse.

Susan Grabowski was unsure of what awaited her as she made her way to the office. She had cooled down considerably but could not deny her lingering anger. Fear for the job she had just begun to love again crept into her mind. Could she blame a twelve-year-old for her own actions? Johnny was difficult, but she was a professional and was supposed to protect students. As she entered the office, Johnny's sad and tearful eyes met her own. This was not the angry boy who spat on her desk.

The simple question couldn't wait for Principal Adams' presence.

"Why?"

With pain and regret etched deeply on his face, his quivering lips softly responded.

"You don't understand. Everybody hates me."

"You're my favorite teacher."

Johnny paused and took another breath.

"And even you hate me."

He looked at her with the most desperately tired eyes she had ever seen.

"Please just leave me alone."

His face fell into his hands as he began to cry again.

Being alone was the last thing he wanted. There was no hesitation or thought as she slid her arms around the student she had undeniably hated earlier that day. He was a student in pain. Susan would never see Johnny as a monster again. There had to be an answer.

Moments later Principal Adams entered the room to find the pair embraced in a comforting hug. There was a lot of work to do, but this was a good start.

CHAPTER 6

The Six Ps Attachment Strategies
Rewiring the Brain

When a person's physiology is balanced (homeostasis), they are relaxed, and as such, they are prepared for new adventures, challenges, and learning. It is not quite so easy for those governed by unhealthy attachments because false-self stories dominate what they know and shape the way they experience the world. Emotional addiction drags them deeper yet, as massive endorphin swings of the addictive drive corrupt neural networks responsible for reward. In both cases, dysregulated neural pathways, chemical imbalance, and dysfunctional beliefs align perfectly with a life of emotional pain.

Disconnected children dream of a life void of anxious feelings and self-doubt. If they had the skills and knowledge to change things on their own, they would have. For others, healthy connections remain at such a distance they may not even know a problem exists. This is an incredibly sad scenario, and these children need help. They need an expert with the proper tools to repair and rebalance neural networks. They need an emotional attachment engineer. This is not a metaphorical statement.

In the most rudimentary sense, that is exactly what being a good parent or teacher has always been. They manage or influence environments, activities, thought patterns, and the emotional energy of experiences, all with the expectation of healthy attachments that set the framework for a happy, healthy life ahead. They probably do not think about chemical balance, changes to neural connectivity and patterning, or healthy endorphin payoffs, but that is exactly what they are doing. They are building or repairing a better healthier brain.

IMPLEMENTING A PURPOSEFUL CONNECTEDNESS INTENTION

From a therapeutic and philosophical perspective, the target is simple. Set a measurable daily intention that enhances the learning experience and ends with a healthy emotional payoff and attachment. Connection and healthy brain development remains a "use it or lose it" proposition, and a defined intention is a proclamation to "use it." Today I will behave, think, or feel this way. The intention has to be clearly defined and achievable. Partial commitment to connection objectives leaves room for avoidance. The addictive drive loves to exploit this opportunity. Anything short of full committal sends mixed messages that breed confusion, increase anxiety, and potentiate unhealthy emotional payoffs and attachments.

It is easy for a person suffering from addiction to drugs, food, or gambling to begin the day with the goal to embrace healthy thoughts and avoid dysfunctional behaviors. It is another matter to make it happen. An achievable target must accompany a manageable plan to prepare for the unhealthy feelings, thoughts, and behaviors the addictive drive will inevitably employ to scuttle their objectives. An immersive connected experience combined with a reduction in addictive distractions or triggers increases the probability of a healthy emotional experience and outcome. The strategy is no different for children in the classroom hamstrung by chronic false-self beliefs.

Teachers want learning to feel good, and they use learning strategies promoting social interactions, sharing, and learning challenge to nurture connections, but in the very real battle to cover curriculum, implementation can become piecemeal or random in nature. Emotionally balanced children can usually manage reasonably well in a scenario like this, but others may need a far more targeted approach. Connection intentions need to be a big deal, immersive, and have a specific purpose. Every experience leaves its mark on neural networks. An emotional attachment engineer does not leave things to chance. Repairing an unhealthy attachment is much more difficult than nurturing healthy ones.

> *"The same experiential and social factors that profoundly shape the brain in early life can also be instrumental in repairing the causes and symptoms of stress related disorders."*
>
> *(Santa Barbara Graduate Institute Center for Clinical Studies and Research, n.d.)*

ENGINEERING AUTHENTIC ATTACHMENTS: IT'S EASY AS ONE-TWO-THREE

When planning lessons, take a step back from curricular objectives and return to the classroom takeaways that really matter. Healthy feelings, thoughts, and behaviors are an excellent start. Take another step deeper beyond reputations, behaviors, or dysfunction. Think how past experiences have influenced brain circuitry in a negative way. Can a teacher rebalance a child's brain and rewrite past stories? Do not panic. It's all about the brain, but it is not brain surgery. A simple Six Ps One-Two-Three connection intervention helps teachers and students make the shift from a passive to active approach for connected learning outcomes.

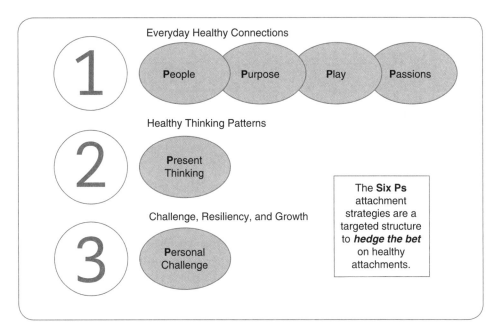

SIMPLE EVERYDAY HEALTHY CONNECTIONS

Simple everyday connections lay the groundwork for connected learning experiences. Teachers can use the first four Ps (People, Purpose, Play, and Passions) to infuse healthy emotional payoffs into everyday lessons. Feel-good experiences are exercise for neural networks that support healthy emotions and biochemical

Simple, Everyday Authentic Connections (People, Purpose, Play, Passions)

- Integrate feel-good connections into daily lessons.

- Learn, practice, and assess connection skills.

- Doing and feeling creates belief: It nurtures a story of competence, contribution, safety, and belonging.

- Connection skills build authentic, supportive culture.

balance. They are also the stepping-stone for connection skill acquisition and building supportive cultures. As a collective whole, the first four Ps write the first chapter in a new believable story.

Learning is supposed to be a pleasurable, fun, and attractive endeavor children look forward to each day. The value of learning and social challenge can quickly disappear if children cannot rebalance. The intention of everyday healthy connections is to make this a reality by triggering the endorphin payoffs that make learning and social interactions feel good. Wrap lessons in authentic exchanges and practice connection skills. Freely smile, laugh, support, and contribute in meaningful ways. Small things matter. They supercharge curricular learning with motivating feel-good emotions. Endorphin payoffs are money in the "emotional bank" and lay a foundation of safety and support for greater challenges ahead.

Most learning and healthy attachments are not a response to intense challenge or emotional trauma. They are a product of everyday, connected moments and emotional payoffs. When these small but frequent experiences become an immersive and normalized part of a child's everyday life, a believable true-self story of safety, belonging, and purpose is painted. If those experiences and the feelings that come with them are vividly clear and acknowledged as favorable events, attachments to those beliefs and feelings are forged. It has always been nature's plan for learning to be playful and pleasurable.

Baby Steps of Connection

In a perfect world, simple, authentic connections would never be a challenging or painful endeavor. A hug is normally a wonderful gesture, but for some children a simple touch, greeting, or conversation can be truly difficult. A seemingly insignificant attempt at an authentic moment can trigger survival mode because, big or small, connection is always a threat to the addictive drive and a stress response is how it fights back. In the world of addiction, small is a relative term. Baby steps are more in order. Everyday healthy connections begin with simple, nonthreatening definable connected behaviors and skill sets. Anxious children may find a step-by-step or paint by numbers approach more manageable. When children are not ready for the thinking part of connection, the doing part must be simple.

In the beginning stages of a connection intervention, success is key. It is the nature of the addictive drive to make connection an uncomfortable, confusing experience marked by anxiety, doubt, and failure. That is why we have to take the time to break skills down to the basics and make sure children have clear standards set for what quality connections look like. Small and specific achievable tasks are easily measured. Vague fluff words like empathetic, kind, and leadership are confusing and easily avoided. Smiles and voice tone are a more reasonable starting point than a broad bravery objective or a challenging complex task at the front of the class. Small achievable tasks are less likely to trigger pushback from powerful addictive attachments that tell students they cannot do something. The payoffs will probably not change the world, but as skill sets grow, so will the occurrence and power of modest but numerous, feel-good connected moments. A science teacher uses the connection checklist below (see Figure 6.1) to encourage and assess connections during cooperative labs. Healthy feelings are evidence of healthy attachments.

FIGURE 6.1

Pinetree Science Teamwork Checklist

Leader:_____

Team Players always know:

- that partners work together. Leaders support; they are *not* the boss;
- to help or receive help graciously;
- that helping partners perform their best and feel positive about the experience is rewarding;
- they have a responsibility to learn lab procedure or course content so they can help others;
- procedure and safety protocols are everyone's responsibility (you are responsible for each other); and
- to not be satisfied with your poor performance or work habits. Set high standards, and take positive action!

Check	Positive Teamwork Behaviors
	• **Smile a lot!**
	• **Use names** if possible (you can ask—it shows personal interest).
	• **Look others in the eyes** to gather attention and make a connection.
	• **Give compliments** (try a *compliment sandwich*—good effort but try to refer to the example in your notes-that's-it-way to go!).
	• **Model the correct steps** by doing it with them, using the mini white board.
	• **Use the word** *we* or other team words often—"We can do this. This is a great group!"
	• **Take the time to help partners** if they struggle. They will appreciate it.
	• **Be intuitive**—read others body posture, voice tone, and energy level. It might be important to how you proceed.
	• **Be a CHEERLEADER!** Catch people doing great things—hi-fives and celebrations.

Check off all the leadership actions that you performed on the above list. Score yourself out of a hundred. This should reflect your overall performance regarding setting and expecting high standards, sharing energy, and most important, making positive connections with your peers. Consider this mark with a "Proud" factor. Are you feeling good that you helped others in a positive way? Don't expect to be in the 90s on your first try—this takes practice but is very rewarding once you have it.

Score ____/100
What I was really good at _____
Areas to improve on_____

SOURCE: Vanessa Martino, 2018 (personal communication)

When teachers prioritize and integrate connection skills and authentic objectives into math, science, or language lessons, they are subtly forcing the creation of new reputations and beliefs. It is a challenge for a child to embrace a bully persona when the class is celebrating positive language. It is hard to believe you have no friends when you engage daily with others in positive ways. An actual experience may prove playing with a friend is more rewarding than a smart phone obsession. Authentic daily experiences are indisputable proof of truth. It feels good to be connected. Everyday connected moments are how teachers can prove that. Prioritizing connection skills in lessons also elevates the importance of connection as a major educational objective. The simple skills and beliefs that emerge lay the foundation for Steps Two and Three of the Six Ps attachment strategies.

HEALTHY THINKING PATTERNS AND THE STATEMENT OF SAFETY

The first four Ps (People, Purpose, Play, and Passions) suggest actions or connected circumstances capable of triggering a healthy emotional response. The fifth P (Present thinking) is different and relates to living in the moment, positive thinking, mindfulness, and truth. The emotional payoff comes from the sense of control individuals feel when they can effectively manage the circumstances of the moment.

Present Thinking Patterns: Protect us from anxious stories and push us toward truth. I will be OK!

- Grounding in TRUTH and sense of self

- Recognize the difference between purposeful stress and unnecessary anxious emotions

- Mindfulness and relaxation strategies

- Anticipate and prepare for emotional challenge

- Connected perspective—Challenge is difficult: Value and celebrate it!

- Gives ownership for one's own sense of safety

IMAGE SOURCE: Courtesy of Amber Geremia

Present thinking represents the cognitive part of connection and an attachment to *truth*. The way children think and process anxious feelings has a significant influence on how learning experiences and emotions are processed. Healthy thinking gives children the power to choose connection when the addictive drive and anxiety is telling them not to.

Healthy thinking patterns give ownership for one's own emotional state and sense of safety. This strategy is useful for teaching children to think their way out of unnecessary stress and the untrue frightening stories anxiety creates. It is particularly important for children who blame others or circumstances for their emotional distress. Look to the fifth P for intention ideas that give children control over their own emotions and destiny.

A statement of safety is an important opening activity in the Emotionally Connected Classroom lesson plan. It is a proclamation that provides grounding and protects students from anxious false-self stories. Its weapon of choice is truth. Children deeply connected with who and what they are cannot be traumatized by trivial name-calling or failure of a test in the way that a disconnected child may. They recognize anxious physiological responses as unnecessary, anticipate emotional roadblocks, and respond with healthy thinking patterns and behaviors allowing them to relax, rebalance, and embrace the learning task. They also know how to process authentic experiences or challenges in the most powerful Good Wolf ways.

Grounding in Truth

Regardless of how emotionally and physically safe a classroom feels, the addictive drive will always attempt to create stories that say otherwise. It can easily project fearful possibilities in the future and recall drama from the past as it attempts to sabotage lessons designed to nurture connected moments. However, it does have a difficult time existing and perpetuating false stories when a child chooses to examine the truth and safety of the present moment.

This is where teachers can build on the everyday healthy connections they have nurtured and use them as proof to ground children in present moment truth. If things get difficult, children with weaker connections to personal safety and belief in a supportive culture may need help with directions to their safe place. When the anxious responses of learning challenges inevitably attempt to create stories that threaten feelings of safety, pulling back to the present moment and taking an inventory of truth can settle unnecessary emotions. The backbone of resiliency is a strong attachment to healthy personal beliefs and present moment truth.

Healthy thinking patterns in learning begin with emotional awareness. When it comes to anxious feelings, it is important to recognize the source of discomfort.

Anxious feelings resulting from family problems, health issues, social challenges, or grades have little to do with the learning experience ahead. They are unnecessary, and moving ahead with a lesson will nurture an attachment between unhealthy emotions and learning. It is unreasonable to expect a child to embrace and succeed at a challenging learning endeavor until the underlying stress issue is resolved. "I'm not ready" is an acceptable response when accompanied by mindfulness strategies like breathing or a walk in nature to remedy the scenario before moving ahead with learning.

Anxious feelings specific to the learning experience have value and get different treatment. Eliminating them is not the objective. It is about embracing *uncomfortable*, valuing it as a means of growth or healing and preparing thought patterns to deal with the challenge. A big part of emotional preparation is an acceptance that challenge is difficult, uncomfortable, and inevitable. The emotional reward is different from the feel-good payoffs of simple connections. They have to be earned, are buried beneath discomfort, and will be delayed. On the surface, this might not sound too appealing to an anxious child. The promise of an exhilarating and rewarding experience must be compelling.

THE PE FITNESS TEST: A TRUTHFUL PERSPECTIVE

Years later, when people think back to what they hated about school, physical education (PE) is often the center of attention, and the dreaded fitness test comes to the top of the list. Virtually all the disgruntled participants willingly admit that the fitness challenge was good for them, but the experience never felt that way. The athletes shared a smirk and a wink, because top scores were a guarantee. Others could think only of physical discomfort and judgment defining them as out of shape, weak, or quitters. They couldn't help but believe their best effort would end in another C grade or less. For them, PE stood for public embarrassment. The physical pain of the task may be what they remember as unpleasant, but a true reflection will reveal it is the feelings of shame and "less than" that has lingered.

TRY THIS!

Engage in a physical task that pushes known limits and feels physically uncomfortable or painful (not dangerously so, of course): Emotional pain and unhealthy thoughts often accompany physical challenges. An advantage of an uncomfortable physical task is that physical pain goes away when it is over. It is no longer necessary in the same way that lingering emotional discomfort is also unnecessary. Physical challenge is a great opportunity to practice letting go of emotional pain and unhealthy thoughts of failure. Arm students with thought patterns that help anticipate, manage and rebalance the emotions that accompany the experience. Celebrate growing resiliency.

Mr. Stevens

Reworking Discomfort

"Everybody wants to be their best. Best efforts and overcoming difficulty always feels amazing. It is the same for all, but another truth also exists. Challenge and our best always come with the price of discomfort. Today I am asking you to embrace amazing over discomfort.

"The run will be uncomfortable but something else very specific will happen to you. Anxiety thrives in the world of discomfort, and at some point during the test its voice will pay you a visit. It will use the discomfort you experience to paint an attractive story that tells you to reduce your efforts and perhaps even quit. Listen and you will experience relief and feel better, but that is a lie. Maybe it will be true for a moment, but inevitably, feelings of shame and guilt will follow when you realize the choice to be less than your best does not feel good. I don't like to use those words, but the truth is, anxiety fights dirty.

"Today, the number of laps you run will not determine your grade. I am going to give you a specific thinking task to assess and reflect on. Recognize the uncomfortable feelings of effort as a normal part of challenge. Know they are temporary and will soon go away. Most important of all, say "No!" to anxiety and the story it tells. Choose your story of champion. Celebrate perseverance, and I promise you will feel amazing. Give yourself a score out of a hundred that reflects how wonderful you feel about your thinking efforts."

PE gets the often unfair but understandable bad rap as the most uncomfortable part of many students' educational experience. But pain is pain whether it is emotional or physical. Stress responses happen in all subject areas, and children need to learn to manage them and perhaps even take advantage of the experience just the same. Presentations or tests are obvious culprits, but it could happen in a math, science, or art class when hard work ends up not working out at all. It is disappointing, but the successful ones learn from mistakes and get better rather than dwelling on them. From a teacher's perspective, it is much easier to prepare students for uncomfortable emotions than it is to clean up a mess of unhealthy feelings and lasting attachments. This is why frontloading and valuing healthy thinking patterns as an important assessable concept for the learning process is always important in lesson planning.

- *Failure is awesome! It is proof you were brave and tried something really hard.*

- *If a task feels easy and comfortable, it really isn't a challenge.*

- *Uncomfortable feelings are a signal that effort or bravery was present and worthy of celebration.*

- *Difficult means you are pushing beyond what you already know or can do.*

- *Learning and emotional challenge is an opportunity for growth and healing.*

- *Stress or discomfort is temporary. Choose to let it go!*

PERSONAL CHALLENGE, RESILIENCY, AND GROWTH

Left to their own devices, the disconnected typically choose easy and avoid authentic challenge. After all, challenge is uncomfortable and a threat to the false-self stories they believe to be true. "I can't so I shouldn't try" sounds like a reasonable and justified coping strategy for someone who believes challenge feels bad. Children have to want change and believe their hard work will feel good in the end. Perhaps the most powerful way to tip the scales in favor of the homeostatic drive and healthy attachments during learning challenge is to put it where it naturally belongs. Turn challenge into purposeful, supportive play, and passionate adventures. Suddenly stressful experiences become less scary and far more manageable.

The most pivotal moments in life, for good or bad, are the product of emotionally charged experiences. Shifts to neural network patterning can be profound, immediate and lasting. The sixth P (Personal Challenge) embraces challenge and anxiety itself as a tool for emotional alignment, healing and growth. Use this strategy when engaging in stressful learning experiences or challenging, unhealthy false-self beliefs.

3 *Personal Challenge: An attachment will always occur. Hedge the bet on a healthy one.*

- Use emotional challenge to write a connected healthy story.

- Wrap the challenge in authentic connections, healthy thinking, support, and celebration (the other five Ps).

- Monitor emotional energy, adapt, and reflect.

Many of the most powerful attachments happen during or after trauma. The attachment can be unpredictable. One person may come out emotionally scarred while another emerges stronger than ever because of the challenge. The outcome for the disconnected is almost a certainty. In the classroom, one would hope that stress is somewhat more predictable and manageable. Teachers can take a proactive approach and use the stress, recovery, attachment process in a healthy advantageous way. The more connected and supported children are, the greater the degree of readiness for learning challenge, risk, and emotional healing. Challenge, be it emotional, physical, or learning-based, will end in some kind of attachment. Tip the scales in favor of a healthy one by pulling all the pieces together. Managing anxious emotions is not a tool of avoidance. It is a strategy for growth. Intentions related to personal challenge help students value and embrace the world of *uncomfortable* in healthy ways. Use present moment truth strategies to recognize and manage unnecessary stress. The feel-good payoffs of People, Purpose, Play, and Passions supply the motivation and support to persevere.

THINK ABOUT IT

Learning is a whole series of effectively managed little emotional traumas that turn out for the best.

Unnecessary stress, by definition, has no purpose and comes with dangerous downside of unhealthy attachments. Healthy stress is different because it always has a purpose. It is always targeting an unhealthy attachment or forging a new one that is a part of the normal maturation process.

Emotional challenge can be a powerful pivotal moment in a child's life. It does not matter if the perceived trauma, planned or unplanned, is large or small, a lasting attachment will occur. It is time for teachers to empty their emotional toolbox and stack the deck for a healthy attachment. The first five Ps of connection remind us of those feel-good behaviors and thoughts that help children experience challenge from a more rewarding perspective. Wrap challenge and learning in things that feel good. Prove the Bad Wolf stories are unfounded and the anxious emotions that come with them unnecessary. When children are learning from a place of purpose, have healthy coping skills at their side, and have peers to cheer them on, it is much harder for false-self attachments and the addictive drive to be the coping strategy of choice.

UNNECESSARY STRESS

Too often the purpose of learning challenges is nothing more significant than a grade with little long-term meaning or relevance. The attachment that follows the potentially anxious experience matters far more, but is not normally given the consideration it deserves. It can be carried for a long time to come and will influence other experiences in a good or bad way. Challenge can be a turning point in the lives of children if it is purposeful. Stress without purpose or a plan for emotional recovery is an unnecessary risk.

THINK ABOUT IT

Are we consciously planning for healthy attachment outcomes in stressful moments? Does the stress have purpose?

- Testing

- Class Presentations

- Physical Challenges

- Competitions

- Social Interactions

Thinking about stress and survival responses does not mean absolute avoidance. That would also mean passing up opportunities to challenge unhealthy attachments that children live with in their daily lives. By intentionally triggering anxious responses related to false-self attachments, teachers are targeting fear, anger, or "less than" beliefs and the unhealthy coping strategies and behaviors that accompany them. Of course, the caveat is that children cannot be "stressed-out" and left hanging with anxious emotions. The process must come full circle to a relaxed balanced state if a new story and healthy attachment is to be the outcome. The complete process of stress to relaxed balanced states is an unconditional requirement for healthy outcomes. Stressing children out and hoping for the best is not a plan.

ASSESSING CONNECTION INTENTIONS AND ONE-TWO-THREE STRATEGIES

In an environment where grading and competition have always been king, who really cares about a smile or laugh? Assessment or reflections elevate the status of connection intention objectives and help students stay true to those intentions throughout lessons. They provide an opportunity to relive or emote emotions that prove the learning experience was a meaningful and worthwhile endeavor. Reflections or assessments are most effective when perceived as a big deal.

Many socioemotional competencies use check box type rubrics or assessments that measure actions or behaviors with descriptive phrasing such as works well with others, self regulates emotions, demonstrates empathy, listens to others opinions, or demonstrates leadership. Vague and wide-scoped phrasings followed by *the student does this* (e.g., never, sometimes, often, or always) are misleading. When it comes to assessment, it is easy to forget that socioemotional competencies should be about feelings and the desire and choice to repeat healthy behaviors in the future rather than the acts themselves.

Meaningful assessment identifies the reasons a child engages in any particular behavior. Are they helping others for authentic intrinsic reasons or are they doing it because a teacher tells them to, for peer approval, or for a specific grade? Potentially, a student could get a check in the *always helps others* box and end up with a positive assessment even though the motivation to repeat the behavior in the future may not exist at all.

Some teaching models use complex rubrics at the end of lessons or units to measure multiple learning tasks or behaviors with a more *must be better* perspective. The more targets, boxes, or scores, the more accurate the assessment. That may be true if the teacher is focusing on product-based assessments. Intentions related to process or feelings need to be simple. A child cannot target bravery, contribution, play, effort, healthy thinking, and communal safety all at once in a meaningful way. Too many authentic targets are unachievable and will likely become hoop-jumping tasks for marks rather than an accurate measure of feeling and belief. For connection assessment, less is usually more.

When deciding on the type of connection assessment format best suited for a class, be it grades, percentage, competencies, portfolios, reflections, or any other type of assessment, purpose is the first consideration. Typically, formative is most suitable because the process of nurturing attachments and neural alignment is never finite. It is always ongoing, and as life and education progress, no tick mark or grade will make it a completed task.

Authentic assessment of a connection intention begins with measuring the desire and capacity to choose connection followed by honest reflection upon how the choice and experience made them feel. A connection intention is nothing if the choice to embrace it as their own comes without commitment. The combination of choice and commitment is a definable measure of *trying*. Reflecting on feelings related to the task can strengthen the bond between trying, effort, and learning. In the best-case scenario, the assessment will be a declaration that the experience changed a belief. "That learning experience felt good, and I want to do it again." An authentic low score or reflection is equally valuable, because it is an acknowledgment that a more focused effort or committed choice is possible and may provide the foundation for a new plan tomorrow. Both outcomes are truthful and reflective of a growth mindset.

When used as a tool for changing belief systems, authentic assessment of connection intentions creates evidence that being a bully, a shy kid, or a failure is not the only option. "Feel Good" I am enthusiastic, I am funny, I am positive, I am resilient, I am a contributor, and I am a learner outcomes may represent a measurable shift. Feelings and choice are a better assessment target because they prove beliefs are changing and a new or stronger attachment to connections and growth is emerging.

The figure below is an assessment tool that can be used to measure commitment to intentions. This type of assessment, in whole or in part, can quantify singular daily intentions, a set of intentions for a unit, or a term review of personal growth. A "**WOW!**" outcome is the home run of connected learning.

1 Developing (**D**) 2 Commits (**C**) 3 Fully Commits (**FC**) 4 **WOW!** An experience felt amazing or changed a belief				
Personal Growth	**I Choose to:**			
	• Take risks & value mistakes	➤ **D**	**C**	**FC**	*WOW!*
	• Challenge my weaknesses	➤ **D**	**C**	**FC**	*WOW!*
	• Set high standards for myself	➤ **D**	**C**	**FC**	*WOW!*
	• Honestly reflect upon my efforts	➤ **D**	**C**	**FC**	*WOW!*
	• Be responsible for my participation	➤ **D**	**C**	**FC**	*WOW!*
Purpose	**I Choose to:**			
	• Share positive energy	➤ **D**	**C**	**FC**	*WOW!*
	• Value what others do and say	➤ **D**	**C**	**FC**	*WOW!*
	• Be a great peer coach	➤ **D**	**C**	**FC**	*WOW!*
	• Practice connection skills and language	➤ **D**	**C**	**FC**	*WOW!*
	• Think team success and cooperation	➤ **D**	**C**	**FC**	*WOW!*
Healthy Thinking	**I Choose to:**			
	• Embrace positive thoughts emotions	➤ **D**	**C**	**FC**	*WOW!*
	• Value discomfort and effort	➤ **D**	**C**	**FC**	*WOW!*
	• Value who I am	➤ **D**	**C**	**FC**	*WOW!*
	• Challenge unhealthy emotions/beliefs	➤ **D**	**C**	**FC**	*WOW!*
	• Own my experiences and emotions	➤ **D**	**C**	**FC**	*WOW!*

NOTE: *I choose to* is different than *I can*. *I can* is a measure of capacity to do or mimic but not necessarily proof of desire or healthy attachment. *I choose to* is symbolic of ownership of an intention.

Teachers do not have to accept anxious beliefs, behaviors, and an inability to cope or learn as a child's truth, because they are not. Curriculum is a very small part of learning, yet it consumes the greatest amount of a teacher's time and energy. Fortunately, in a truly connected classroom, connection is not the responsibility of teachers alone. They have an incredible resource right in front of them. The next chapter takes a closer look at how the emotional engineer facilitates, nurtures, and employs supportive cultures to do the job for them.

The Refugee Camp: Survival, Choices, and Resiliency

Fine brown dirt swirled about as each tired step disrupted the once lush countryside. The same hot dry wind that carried the dust away sapped his energy and left him in a constant state of thirst. The drought and the war had worked together in a perfect storm to tear his beautiful world apart. He had been carrying the bucket of dirty water for 40 minutes, and it would be at least that long before he arrived at his home in the refugee camp. He had plenty of time to think about his new life.

Things had been difficult, but his remaining family was alive and with him. The danger he faced alone in forest now seemed insignificant compared to the terrors they endured on their 3-week trek to the refugee camp. Traveler stories of murder and rape struck fear into their hearts and left them with sleepless nights despite their relentless fatigue. Fears were realized the night bandits stole what little possessions and food that remained.

Inubu tried desperately to stop them, but a gun in his mouth quickly nullified his pathetic attempt. He doubted the memory of cold steel rattling against his teeth would ever leave him. Days later, weakened by hunger and illness, Inubu and his mother finally took their last desperate steps into the camp. His younger brother was emaciated, unnaturally bloated, and near death. Compassionate care workers gave them food, water, and medical attention. Their kindness gave him hope that the entire world had not gone mad.

They were lucky. Many of the villagers never made it to the camp. He often found himself scanning the flat plain hoping to see them, but like the dust, those hopes blew away with the relentless wind.

He was grateful for the relative safety of the camp, but life remained a challenge. There was never enough food, and people often fought over the meager resources found. Little hope existed here as desperation filled the hearts and minds of the tired inhabitants. Still, endless streams of refugees flowed into the already overcrowded camp each day.

Boys, at one time his good friends, succumbed to gang pressure to become thieves who stole from the starving and sold drugs to the already lost. When he refused to join their ranks, threats and bullying became a part of his daily commute home from the camp's temporary school. Worse yet, promises of food and a modest salary drove others to find a new home with the militant groups that had started the war, destroyed their villages, and ruthlessly murdered their loved ones. This was a world he could not understand and fought with absolute resolution not to.

The journey back from the water hole was nearing its end, and just ahead lay the ramshackle tent called home. Random pieces of plastic and discarded wood supported a faded blue tarp with ragged edges. It wasn't much, but this was the place where his mother's warm hugs and his little brother's contagious smiles ended his day on a high. There was no campfire, but they still shared the stories of their days and sang joyful songs together, just as they had always done in their village. The screams of his mother shattered the thoughts of the pleasant moment.

The bucket of water he had painstakingly carried exploded as it hit the ground. No door on the tent hid the man that pushed his mother to the ground. Rage boiled over as he watched the intruder collect their meager rations in his arms. Inubu grabbed a heavy stick he kept beside the entrance and swung with all his might. With a sickening crack, the wood splintered across the back of the unsuspecting man's head. Dazed, he rolled across the dirt floor onto his back. A knife from their makeshift kitchen had already found the boys hand and its point was centered on the evil man's throat.

His eyes widened with shock as he looked into a face that was immediately recognized. Rage, fear, and confusion collided in an explosion of overwhelming emotion. In the village this man traded fairly with his father and treated Inubu and his brother kindly with animated stories of the city. It wasn't unusual for a rare candy treat to round off his visits.

He was only a boy. He had been through so much, and it felt like his mind was breaking. Anger pushed the blade harder upon the throat of the man who dared not breathe. Droplets of deep red blood appeared along the sharp knife-edge. Time slowed as the pressure on the knife continued to rise. A fearful but calming voice found Inubu's ear.

"Your father would not want you to become one of them."

The memory of his father was powerful. It was just enough to save the man's life. Inubu withdrew, and the broken man staggered out of the tent. He turned to his traumatized mother, and again she softly spoke.

"It is as my dead brother foretold. You are indeed a brave warrior."

With trembling arms wrapped around his mother, they quietly wept together for some time.

Alertness and fear unexpectedly returned as the sound of footsteps running toward the tent crushed the peaceful moment. Inubu took a deep breath and reached for the knife.

His tension melted and he let out a deep sigh of relief as his smiling brother bounced into the hut. He was excited to tell them about the goals he scored in the pretend World Cup football match with his friends. Love for the child and his beautiful joyful face pulled Inubu and his mother back from their state of despair as they returned his smile and listened intently. The lovely little boy would never learn of the matter that had happened only moments before.

CHAPTER 7

Drug Addicts, Gamblers, Classrooms, and Dogs

An odd chapter title, but the point is simple. All humans, regardless of our situation or possible dysfunction, are significantly influenced by the emotional energy of those who surround us. This communal energy has shaped who we are in the past and will largely determine the path our life takes in the future. Humans are pack animals, having evolved to depend on connections with our family, friends, and community for emotional balance. We are extremely sensitive to the energy of our pack. Those closest to us have the greatest potential to nurture feelings of love, safety, support, and balance. They may also be our greatest source of emotional pain. In the classroom, *pack energy* will be a major player in any connection intervention.

Dale is a therapy dog who comes to school with his teacher friend on Wednesdays. He cannot speak, give advice, or share a story that will make things better. However, intuitively drawn to students in distress, he is capable of sharing his own healthy relaxed energy to help make his human pack feel better.

IMAGE SOURCE: Photo of Dale by Ian Wong, reproduced courtesy of Derek Wintermans

ADDICTION INTERVENTIONS

The classic interventions for drug abusers, alcoholics, gamblers, or those suffering from food addictions often demonstrate a similar pattern. The family or support group gather together to share their concerns and, with the aid of the interventionist, put together a plan to address the addiction. This may include a stint in a rehabilitation center where the loved one can rebalance in a safe environment and learn coping strategies to manage the challenge ahead.

Problems arise when he returns to the community or environments that may have played a significant role in the emotional disconnection that lies at the heart of his addiction. An overprotective mother and a demanding father with anger issues might not offer the reliable source of healthy emotional energy the teen addicted to drugs or an eating disorder needs. Inconsistency and anxious energy is confusing for a person searching for a path back to emotional balance.

Other scenarios are less dramatic and involve highly motivated loving family or friends. They want to help but may not know how and might be unaware of the subtler emotional drama in which they unconsciously play a part. Even relatively connected support groups need to hone connection skills and be aware of the truthful emotional energy they project. Caring and love may not be in question, but they flow much more freely from balanced people with truthful connected perspectives. Efforts to ensure support groups are balanced and emotionally ready to share healthy energy with others is key. Anxiety and stress are contagious. Fortunately, so are smiles, joy, and love.

EDUCATED SUPPORT GROUPS

People living with addiction face hurdles that others do not. They cannot see clearly in the way that connected people do. The uncomfortable emotional highs and lows they experience drive them further from truth, and they consciously or unconsciously try to take loved ones along for the ride. Emotionally balanced support groups demonstrate clarity of thought and are in a position to expose the lies of addiction and to offer a more connected alternative. The more connected the support group, the greater the stability and influence to create a new story grounded in truth.

Love and trying hard is not enough. Blind support will inevitably end in random results. Kindness, caring, and patience could easily mutate to enabling. Likewise, imposed, firm structure with the authentic intention to manage behaviors can lead to intense emotional control dramas. Educated connected support means recognizing unhealthy attachments and emotions, demonstrating the awareness to avoid feeding the Bad Wolf, and having a plan to forge healthy attachments. The irrational nature of addiction is challenging because it fears connection and will always push loved ones away. Educated connected support groups are resilient and ready for this.

At some point, life will go sideways for all people. It is part of our evolutionary blueprint to depend on our pack to help us rebalance. Support makes us feel good and safe and allows us to get back on course. This plan is an evolutionary success story. However, the strategy falls short if people are not motivated to support others. This is why evolution made supporting those we love or care about the most authentic and powerful payoff we may ever experience.

What if children had the skill sets and connected beliefs to influence the lives of others in the most positive ways possible? The ability to share healthy emotional energy is a powerful asset and empowering scenario. Part of the natural development toward independence is embracing closer connections with peers. There is a natural pressure to be part of the group and embrace similar actions and beliefs. If we assume this as true, steps to ensure peer groups are balanced and have the connection skills to support each other in meaningful and rewarding ways becomes an important part of the peer learning process and experience.

"Fix It" Strategies Don't Work in Anxious Environments

An unbalanced classroom ripe with anxiety, stress, and dysfunction will undoubtedly limit the effectiveness of the coping strategies counselors provide. Emotional addictions and anxiety are quick to take advantage of chaotic environments and nervous energy. Anxiety doggedly searches out the smallest failures in emotional safety net strategies and creates bombastic stories to trigger unnecessary emotional pain. Inevitably, this reduces the credibility of potentially helpful coping strategies counselors provide. The all-important trusting, connected relationship counselors depend on is fragile and always under siege.

This is the challenge for traditional "fix it" approaches aimed at improving the emotional health and wellness of students at school. Even if we begin with the assumption that psychologists and counselors are spot on with the emotional coping strategies provided, a major problem remains. Inevitably, the office door must open and students return to the disconnected environment that may have triggered the dysfunction in the first place. If customizing a balanced safe environment were a viable option, therapists would certainly choose to do so, but in most cases, they have little or no influence over the relaxed supportive conditions needed for a believable sense of safety. Teachers are in a somewhat better position because they have more control over experiences and environments. They can also monitor behaviors and give immediate feedback for support groups.

Much of the current literature and professional development forums support the belief that healthy student–teacher relationships significantly benefit students. This appears to be especially true for at-risk children (Klem & Conell, 2004). Teachers know their capacity to influence is directly proportional to the strength of the connections they share. Undoubtedly, these relationships can help smooth out the bumps when children with no other lifeline struggle, but the pressure for the compassionate teacher to be all things for all students is significant and continues to grow. This may translate into a potentially all-consuming responsibility because the scope of disconnection has become so widespread.

Some energetic teachers do manage to juggle multiple relationships, but they are, at best, a temporary arrangement because students move on to other grades and eventually leave school behind altogether. It would be a ludicrous plan to set a 1-year limitation with your best friend, spouse, or child. Likewise, at-risk students dependent on a single teacher is a temporary solution at best. It is not nature's way to make connectedness for so many the responsibility of one person. Sharing connections should not be a daunting task. A mutually rewarding and enjoyable experience that brings reliable, long-term balance to the lives of students is a far more efficient plan.

PEER CONNECTIONS: THE NATURAL WAY

Infants depend on healthy connections with parents. As they move on to school, teachers share in this responsibility, but as they mature toward independence, peer relationships become dominant in the natural order of things. Two-way, mutually supportive relationships serve as a practice ground for meaningful contribution and discovery of purpose. Peer relationships are a comfortable place to make mistakes and learn connection skills together.

Matters are somewhat different with the student–teacher relationship; an underlying sense that it is always a predominately one-way street remains. The mark of a healthy mature relationship is that both parties grow and benefit from the exchange, but while teachers freely embrace the personal satisfaction of influencing student growth, the reverse is not usually true to the same degree. Students want to influence, coach, and improve the life of others. A peer is a far better fit than a teacher with worldly experience.

Students need peer relationships to learn how to contribute and practice their connection skills as they mature into valued members of society. Without these relationships, there may be a missing piece in their natural development. The big push to build stronger student–teacher connections may be just one more example of doing it for them rather than helping them develop the skills to do it themselves. At best, it is a short-term connectedness Band-Aid. At its worst, it may prove to be a detrimental replacement for the natural peer connections they need.

ALTERNATIVE PEER GROUPS

In the absence of a healthy support group, students inevitably gravitate toward alternative groups that may not be able to provide the type of emotional support needed. Antiestablishment does not necessarily equate to anger or "poor me" emotions and beliefs, but it is a common occurrence. Misery loves company. The natural reaction to this understandable safety concern is to drive a wedge between students and their natural need to connect with each other. This overt disconnection fuels unhealthy emotions and behaviors parents or teachers are specifically trying to avoid. The more parents or teachers try to force unhealthy peer influences apart, the greater the addictive draw becomes. Separating students in classrooms, schools, or communities that parents or teachers believe pose a danger would be an excessively time-consuming task. It is a battle eventually lost anyway.

When looking at problem groups or individuals in the classroom, the first thing a teacher will typically see is the dysfunctional behavior that defines them as a threat. This is a completely normal reaction. We always see behavior or, worse yet reputations, first. If teachers focus on dysfunction or reputation, they will probably miss the all-important true-self connection piece. Every student wants to make the world a better place, influence the lives of others in a positive way, and solidify their own place of safety within a supportive group. Alternative groups are all about support and acceptance. They just may not be very good at it. A better way to deal with the fears associated with these groups is to help them get better at sharing healthy energy and thoughts. Every student's true self is good and wonderful, regardless of history or reputation.

Many of the best counselors, youth workers, or even teachers have come from very troubled pasts. Their own emotional pain they experienced as youths leaves them highly motivated to help others, and they may come from a position of understanding others may not possess. Life's lessons came the hard way. Some may have been fortunate enough to get the support they needed in tough times, while others had to go it alone. Either way, the point remains; they discovered their own truth and were able to shed the burden of their reputations. Dysfunctional groups or individuals within the class can do the same. If we can teach groups to support in healthy ways, there will be no need to waste energy keeping them apart. Balance the pack, and starve the addiction.

Nature is on our side; we have to trust and work with it. Children are supposed to support each other. It is part of their biological makeup for it to feel good. Teachers can fully exploit this evolutionary advantage by cultivating connection skills and nurturing the belief that all students can make a difference and benefit from the experience.

PEER EMPOWERMENT

This might sound therapeutically ambitious for students, but the Six Ps attachment strategy simply mimics what nature intended for emotional balance and learning. Students are emotionally intuitive and capable of authentic support, but a little structured guidance also has a place in the natural order of things. Even young peer groups possess the potential to affect others in ways that should not be underestimated.

During a stressful challenge or learning task, could a peer do this?

1. Recognize anxious emotions in a classmate

2. Nurture feelings of safety: "You'll be ok. I'll help you."

3. Coach skills to help their peers be successful

4. Encourage and correct when things go wrong: "We will get it. Try this."

5. Celebrate effort and achievement: "Way to go. We did it."

6. Link behavior, belief, and feelings: "Feels really great doesn't it?"

A student just practiced connected emotional alignment therapy in a way that a counselor in an office never could. Emotional awareness, connected feedback, emotional support, and a plan for forging healthy attachments. It is more natural and achievable than we think. Formal counseling can come with a negative stigma, but in this scenario, the casual observer would probably interpret the interaction as a common, everyday healthy connection. However, connections like this do not typically just happen. They require conscious practice, intent, and guidance.

Changing the way students think about helping or being helped lays the foundation for mutually rewarding healthy peer relationships. Authentic connections offer a different kind of motivation, free of extrinsic reward or competitive victory. Healthy endorphin reward comes from giving authentic assistance or gracious appreciative acceptance of help. It is a win-win outcome.

It is easy to presume or imagine that a class will always sort itself out into competent overachievers surrounded by struggling peers. The winners will help the losers in a one-way relationship. Embracing such a scenario as truthful serves to reinforce beliefs only top students can help or lead. This suggests a large portion of the class would have to forfeit the payoffs associated with contribution or purpose. A secondary problem with this scenario is that top students may be among the most disconnected. High achieving students are already winning in a competitive environment and may be less motivated to offer authentic support. Why should they change the game?

A better starting point begins with believing all students are capable of meaningful contribution. Positive energy, compliments, encouragement, and smiles have greater payoffs and more influence in learning than simply helping with the details of a math problem. Healthy emotional energy is something every student can share regardless of learning disabilities, health issues, or behavioral dysfunction.

Helping or graciously accepting help is a common intention theme in the Emotionally Connected Classroom. Contributing or supporting others is a purposeful experience. It provides a sense of self-worth and verifiable proof they are valued and belong. The emotional reward part of it is easy to understand. When students get a feel-good taste of contribution, they want more.

Reward for the graciously accepting help portion of the equation is a little more complex and may take purposeful thought to value it fully. The fact that somebody cares enough to help is comforting, but the belief that the exchange is a one-way street may create conditions that suggest a hierarchy of status is emerging. Emotional energy always goes both ways. Those who possess the skills of gracious appreciation make the experience for the helper more rewarding. Making somebody else feel good or better always comes with its own personal reward. In the long-term game, there is great value when people enjoy sharing their thoughts and ideas with a particular person. Access to the knowledge and energy of others makes you a truly important and connected person. Low status for accepting help from others—I don't think so!

Case Studies in Physical Education

Leanne

Leanne entered physical education classes with multiple labels making integration difficult. She had Down syndrome, was nonverbal, and demonstrated limited physical capabilities. Identified as "a runner," the chance of randomly fleeing from class posed a safety concern. Prior integration consisted of a few minutes of sideline activities with a teacher assistant followed by a walk. Peer connections were token or minimal.

IMAGE SOURCE: Courtesy of Chantale Breton and Phil Ramsden

In grade 11, Leanne entered her first Emotionally Connected Classroom environment. The class was prepared with a few safety concerns, but for the most part, their role was simple. Understand that Leanne was like any young girl wanting acceptance, friends, and a sense of value. Students were encouraged to share their own healthy energy in activities and social interactions. Talking to her, smiling, and laughing were priorities.

Special education assistants monitored and viewed progress from a discreet location for two reasons. Fleeing to the perceived safety of her aide was a convenient coping strategy when faced with activities that were new and challenging. The second reason related to her peers. It was important to know they were responsible for Leanne and were more likely to second-guess themselves if Leanne kept looking to her aide for assistance.

Sharing healthy emotional energy is an integral part of an emotionally connected learning experience, and in this regard, Leanne quickly became an asset. Leanne's own emotional energy was infectious. The young girl possessed an exceptional gift. She couldn't communicate with words, but her eyes, smiles, and giggles oozed a pervasive, authentic, and warm sense of gratitude. Peers actively pursued opportunities to share time with Leanne not because they had to, but because it felt good.

Her overt challenges made it easy for peers to shift from competitive to supportive thinking. As a collective whole, an interesting shift in the classroom climate occurred. Supportive language and a spirit of sharing cooperative healthy energy among all class members became the norm as connection skills and intentions largely designed for Leanne became the normal way of business.

Peers challenged her, supported her, and celebrated her efforts. At times, the results were slow, but in the end, outcomes were amazing and profound. Leanne began participating in fitness activities, learned to golf, and played in simple team games. Her contagious smile and deep belly laugh always elevated the emotional climate in the best way possible. Most surprising of all, she began to speak the names of those students closest to her. Enthusiastic classroom celebrations followed emerging words like golf or hello. Leanne had become a valued member of the class in the same way any student would want.

Outside of physical education, the learning assistance center worked hard to build on her new vocabulary. Leanne was soon able to perform simple conversations of hello, goodbye, and thank-you. Her life had changed. This on its own was a great success, but her progress affected her peers in equally profound ways. They knew they made a game-changing difference in another person's life. Imagine if you could sit your class down, look them in the eye, and tell them this:

I want you to think about how a mother would feel, if for the first time in 18 years of silence, her daughter came home from school and said the word Mom. Yesterday that happened, and it is largely because of you.

Multi-Grade Learning Environments

Single-grade learning may be convenient for sequential curriculum scaffolding, but it has never been a natural way to learn. Young students advance quicker and learn social skills when they observe and receive support of older students (Vygotsky, 1978). Older students gain deeper understanding in the role of teacher.

Another important factor supporting multi-age learning is that older students demonstrate more kindness and compassion toward younger peers (Whiting, 1983).

Case Study

The Time Stealer

Teachers at a local middle school were frustrated with the unending disruptions and conflicts surrounding a struggling student. His behavior ran the full gambit of dysfunction, with bullying, fighting, grandstanding, talking out constantly, lying, and wandering off. To most, he was simply an unhappy angry student and there appeared to be no solutions to manage his behaviors. He was skilled at creating drama and riding the line of behavior that chronically stole time from teachers and his classmates.

The educational experience was plagued with significant time in the office or at home suspensions. He tried desperately to manage his life, but dysfunctional coping strategies continually made life worse. The understandable animosity and frustration directed toward him by many of his teachers and peers offered an unending supply of unhealthy energy to feed his own emotional addictions. He needed a fresh start and new environment.

Administrators from both schools granted permission, and a schedule was set up with the youth worker to bring him to the high school to join a senior fitness class twice a week. This aligned nicely with his goal of becoming a pro football player. It was felt that a senior class would be best suited for a couple of reasons. The first was that bullying and fighting were two of his dominant dysfunctional behaviors, and it was unlikely an eighth grader would be able to create any physical or emotional threat to a high school senior. The second reason addressed his over-the-top "more than," boastful false-self persona. This would have no place and make little sense in a classroom where virtually everybody was larger, faster, more skilled, and certainly more mature. The class was prepared with a brief background and a few key objectives that would help him feel welcome and function in a more reasonable way.

The boy came to meet the teachers before his first day to talk about the exchange and set a few ground rules. He was surprisingly charming and excited at the prospect of joining up with the big guys. It was quite apparent that he needed a break from teachers as much as they needed it from him. Clear expectations were proposed and agreed to.

- *Every behavior is motivated by the intention of making the class better.*

- *Put others first because they will do the same for you.*

- *Every day you will self-evaluate and reflect on your feelings about contributions and effort.*

There were a few awkward moments of inappropriate comments in the early stages, but a little friendly advice from his older classmates quickly steered interactions in a better direction. Over the next several weeks, he embraced modeled behaviors, cheered for others, and challenged himself. He learned that putting down others and his own arrogant self-praise was not nearly as rewarding as celebrations or high fives from others.

One of his most significant growth areas was his ability to honestly and accurately assess and reflect on his feelings and contribution to the class. He scored himself appropriately when he had bad days and was able to communicate a plan for improvement. Despite the occasional hiccup, his daily self-assessments overwhelmingly reflected his belief that he was a valued contributor in the classroom.

He happily shared his positive experiences with his favorite teacher back at middle school. She was very excited to report that he had given a humble presentation to the eighth-grade class on how high school physical education was really hard but fun. Struggles continued at middle school, but teachers noted a significant reduction in bad behaviors and authentic regret often followed missteps. For the first time, they were getting the sense that this student wanted change. There was a spark of hope for the young boy.

TRY THIS!

IMAGE SOURCE: Courtesy of Mona Valdes

When a class is struggling with unhealthy energy and behaviors, consider shaking things up with a multi-grade approach. Team up with an older grade for a fresh peer experience not tied to existing unhealthy emotions. Multi-grade connections have an advantage because they are less likely to have a competitive feel and are more suited to mentorship. A fifth grader will look up to a seventh grader and freely accept help in a way that she would not with a same-grade peer. The immediate change in emotional energy may surprise teachers. Try putting the out-of-balance class in the purposeful mentorship role with a lower grade. Mentoring is a powerful way to reconnect with one's own true self. Arm them with the connection tools and thinking patterns they need and the results may be surprising.

THE EMOTIONALLY CONNECTED CLASSROOM

CONNECTION SKILL SETS FOR MULTI-GRADE LEARNING

For years, schooling, sports teams, and most community activities have created a division of age-exclusive interactions for students. Learning to communicate and interact effectively with different aged peer groups requires skill sets and beliefs many students may not possess. Few have had real opportunities to practice. Big kids may seem scary. Younger ones may seem a nuisance to the older. Getting the most out of multigrade exchanges may take some connection front-loading.

FIFTH-GRADE CREATIVE WRITING ASSIGNMENT (BUT ANY GRADE IS APPLICABLE)

Spice up the creative writing objective. Creating a story for a specific student is a strong motivator for a purposeful experience. Teacher praise or marks are weak creative drivers by comparison.

 TRY THIS!

Creative Writing and Art: The Kindergarten Buddy Class Project

Connection Intentions: Purposefully create a joyful experience for your Kinderbuddy. Practice the skills of connecting with younger peers. Share your story with enthusiasm.

Curricular Objective: Demonstrate creative writing and artwork through an original children's story book.

Pro-tips for creating your Kinderbuddy story:

- Interview your Kinderbuddy. Ask questions to learn about him. What kind of stories does he like? Consider building the story around the strengths of his character.

- Consider simple words and artwork students will understand and bring the story to life. Read age-appropriate children's books to dial in on language level and appropriate topics.

- Give your story a greater purpose by integrating a life lesson.

- Be excited about the opportunity. It will be rewarding!

Pro-tips for sharing your Kinderbuddy story

- Being an older peer comes with responsibility. Your presence will have a significant impact. Value this, and do your best to make it a memorable experience.

- Big kids can be scary. Begin with a gentle and kind welcome. Practice shaking hands. Make a promise that together you will have fun.

- Don't just read your story. Take time and deliver your story with passion and animation.

- The connection and energy shared is more important than the story. Make a friend.

Pro-tips for the Kinderbuddies

- Be excited. You get to have a new Big Friend.

- Be a good listener. People like that!

- Graciously express thanks. Kind words and smiles are a good start. Top it off by creating a thank-you card for your Big Friend.

(Full lesson plan in supplementary materials, pages 188-189.)

PEER CONNECTIONS: NATURALLY SIMPLE

An empowered peer approach for nurturing authentic connections and emotional wellness is efficient because it takes advantage of the collective energy of a community rather than the finite efforts of a single teacher. It aligns with the natural need to connect with peers and provides a backdrop for abundant authentic opportunities and healthy emotional payoffs. It is the way things are supposed to be. "Fix it" approaches and dependence on teacher connections are less efficient and do not make long-term sense. Peer connections make curricular learning more enjoyable and, when utilized in a thoughtful way, double as a natural strategy for nurturing lasting healthy attachments. Even the strongest student–teacher relationships are no substitute for this.

Students spend the vast majority of their day with their peers, and it makes sense for teachers to liberate themselves from labor-intensive responsibilities for student-teacher connections. Students want to support their peers. The more skills they possess, the more pleasurable and influential the experience becomes. Let's return for a moment to our dream classroom: It is always student centered with students laughing and sharing an engaging learning experience together. In this regard, teacher's instincts have always been on point.

Teachers have to deal with the hand they are dealt. Class lists may contain several emotional hot spots with the potential to throw the entire room out of balance. How can teachers let go and delegate responsibility when they are justifiably nervous that peer connections may be counterproductive or even a danger? The next chapter explains the role of relaxed environments and structure in the "how to" for managing anxiety and unhealthy emotional energy. Unhealthy attachments and emotional addiction are formidable adversaries for mutually beneficial peer relationships. Authentic learning structure will help teachers stay the course and expose the true self of even the most chaotic classes.

Ms. Grabowski

A Teacher's Purposeful Plan

"I'm very excited to tell you about a new student who will be joining us tomorrow."

Ms. Grabowski walked toward the large map at the side of the classroom. She pointed to a country most students had never heard of and shared the recent history and turmoil that its people had endured. The bell cut short a lively discussion, and the class shuffled out the door for recess. She caught Johnny's eye and asked him if she could have a moment.

Johnny was confused. He wondered if he was in trouble again, but the warm smile on Ms. G's face lowered his guard.

"I have a special task I would like you to help me with."

Ms. G went into a little more detail on the challenges Inubu was about to face. He had already been through a great deal. Two years in the refugee camp, travelling to a new country, and now he was about to engage in formal education for the first time in his life.

"A warm welcome would certainly ease his worries. How would you feel about showing him around the school?"

Johnny wondered why she chose him. There were better leaders in the class.

CHAPTER 8

Relaxed Environments, Safety, and Structure

Feelings of safety come from healthy attachments to support, self-worth, and present moment truth. Safe feelings allow people to relax, rebalance, and escape the anxious feelings of survival mode.

- I am competent and contribute in meaningful ways.

- I bring value to the greater whole and support others.

- My peers will support me if I fall.

- At the end of the day, school is a safe place, and I will be okay.

- I am in control of my own emotions and life.

Protection, control, and rules are the traditional approach for creating safe environments at school, but in most circumstances, with the exception of truly chaotic dangerous environments, they hamstring authentic attachments and personal accountability for a child's own feelings of safety. Putting safety beyond the control of students through rules and teacher control creates dependency and ultimately raises long-term anxiety.

EVERYBODY NEEDS A SAFE PLACE TO RELAX

Even the most connected people experience unhealthy pressures and need a place to relax, recharge, and rebalance. It would be a terribly boring existence if life never triggered anxiety or stress. Challenge, learning, growth, and life's most exhilarating experiences would be limited without it, but an anxious survival state is not a place where a person wants to remain for any length of time.

If a place or situation is chronically uncomfortable, connected people know to move on. A walk in the park, curling up with a good book in a cozy chair, or sharing a nice dinner with loving family might do the trick and help the stress of the day melt away. Things are not quite so easy for a child. They have little control over their environment, what they do, or whom they do things with. Trading in a dysfunctional family is not an option, and school attendance is compulsory even if it is the primary stressor in a child's daily life.

Stress hormone levels will not return to normal in situations perceived as dangerous or chaotic. Environments that breed conflict, judgment, or isolation keep stress hormone levels high, inhibiting opportunities to rebalance. When children struggle with emotional highs and lows, little energy remains to focus on learning and everyday normal activities. Creating structures and nurturing skills sets that reduce the anxiety of the collective whole is an important first step.

The first day of school is always an anxious experience of the unknown. The emotional baggage some children carry may prove it an overwhelming experience. When the doors open, feelings of judgment and hierarchal status add to the distress. An anxiety therapist would choose a far more relaxed and inviting environment as a place to relax. Some children do make a choice and do not go to school at all.

In competitive school environments, disconnection and emotional addictions have home field advantage. Even the so-called "best kids" are pitted against each other and experience significant stressors. Social competition may be even more challenging. The jocks, popular kids, and academics strive for top status. Delinquents, gang members, and druggies try to find acceptance in unhealthy ways. The nobodies linger in isolation. It is a challenge for any child to find emotional safety and relax at school.

There really isn't any excuse that justifies the anxious and competitive environment that is thrust on children for the vast majority of their day. For the most part, the educational experience of a student lies beyond their control, so there is a justifiable obligation on the part of educators to make it healthy and balanced. In this regard, as a collective whole, the education system has failed miserably.

BELIEF CREATES OUR REALITY

If children feel physically and emotionally safe at school, they almost certainly are. If a reliable, supportive culture exists and the basic emotional needs of a child met, minor mishaps are not really a threat. An unusual exceptional event would have to occur to change that truthful reality in the mind of an emotionally balanced child. However, when chronic anxiety becomes a factor, feelings of safety are always under siege, even in relatively safe environments.

Classroom rules, accountability, and initiatives that promote respectful behaviors set the benchmark for what it means to feel safe at school, but it remains true, even in comparatively safe school environments, anxiety rates remain high. This suggests the vast majority of anxiety triggers lie beyond a dependence on respectful relationships and enforcement of rules. The core issue is not safety, rules, or protection. It is disconnection, lack of resiliency, and anxiety attachments that roam free to create stories of "less than" or danger. The most trivial challenges or speed bumps will suffice. Rules and protection will not change that. Only belief can.

PRESENT THINKING, PROMISES, AND COLLECTIVE INTENTION

There is no such thing as an impenetrable emotional safety bubble teachers can construct and maintain. Anxiety is clever and resourceful. All it needs is a weak link in a child's experiences and belief system to create unsafe feelings. The first and most reliable line of defense for feelings of safety is responsibility for one's own thinking and feelings. Skill sets and attachments supporting present, truthful thinking and mindfulness strategies position children to control their emotional destiny. The most connected can choose to embrace feelings of safety even when the external experience suggests an anxious response. A belief in collective support is the backup when emotions and thoughts inevitably begin to drift.

Where does a teacher start when resiliency attachments are weak and peer groups lack the tools and motivation to support each other? Teachers can begin with a promise, one that makes personal and communal responsibility for safety a priority and the primary driver of all learning. This may be a hard sell when safety, control, and judgment have always belonged to others. A promise may be all a teacher has to offer until experiences prove that another way is possible and true. The new story needs to be vivid, clear, and grounded in hope. Hope is the bridge anxious children need to bravely take that first step into a world of safety that belongs to them.

Promises of safety come with a caveat. They have to be true. Trust is a very fragile matter in the world of the addictive drive. Words and promises may create hope and set a new direction, but anxiety will always fight back and attempt to prove feelings of safety are unfounded. An inadvertent bump during a gym activity, a poor grade on a minor quiz, being the one left without a partner, or a relatively harmless quip from a classmate may serve as a meaningless but effective trigger. This is why a believable promise of safety has to be realistic and not teacher centered. Teachers have significant influence on classroom environments, but they will never be able to guarantee absolute safety of all children. Nor should they try. It is natural for children to look out for each other, but it is hard to do so when teachers dominate the protection and support scene.

A good place to start is an agreed on commitment for personal accountability and a collective intention of safety for all. This scenario offers a healthier proactive perspective than protection. It leaves space for things to go wrong. Protection does not. Protection reinforces a victimized "poor me" reaction and unhealthy payoffs when things inevitably go sideways. It also limits the potential to learn coping skills. Healthy attachments to "I'm okay" or "I am supported" in the face of challenge come with an empowering healthy payoff. This is a far more balancing and rewarding perspective than a dependence on protection from a teacher who may not even know a problem exists.

A STATEMENT OF SAFETY

No responsible teacher would consciously create truly hazardous learning challenges or willingly place children in socially dangerous scenarios. Assuming disconnected children accept this rational perspective as true is never a good idea, and reminding the class to be cognizant of this fact positions them to be sensitive and supportive even in modestly challenging scenarios.

This brings us back to the promises that teachers make about safety. Words are just words until proven by actions and experiences. Anxious emotions are most powerful when they are unexpected, so good teaching will always anticipate and plan for this. Every lesson should begin with a statement of safety that helps children anticipate anxious emotions and sets the groundwork for beliefs and strategies that expose them as unnecessary.

A truthful perspective acknowledges the expectation that anxious emotions will creep into challenging experiences, but there is no need to obsess about them. It is highly unlikely the learning task is life threatening. Failure is only a matter of perspective, and peers will be there to support and make the experience more pleasurable. Anxiety relies on exaggerated, fearful stories in the future or obsessive attachments to unhealthy stories of the past. When children begin to drift and emotionally struggle with Bad Wolf feelings, present truthful thinking and belief in supportive cultures creates the safe haven for emotions grounded in reality.

Mr. Stevens

A Statement of Safety

Today we are going to have some fun canoeing. For those of you feeling a little anxious about a somewhat tippy watercraft, rest assured you are going to be okay. We have learned the skills, I will be nearby if any problems arise, and the lifejacket you wear will keep you safe if all else fails. What's the worst that can happen? The boat flips, you fall in, bob around in the water a few times, we help you out, and then you realize bravery has just earned you a really funny story to share for years to come! That doesn't sound so bad does it? Take a deep breath, and let's have an amazing day.

Do Connected Things in Connected Ways

Doing connected things is one of the best ways to avoid disconnecting ones. When challenging beliefs of the addictive drive, the best defense is a reliable connected offense. When a child is busy sharing and helping others, it is easier to forget about winning, domination, or failure. Practicing present moment thoughts steals the power of disconnecting stories. Still, it is easy for children to fall off track.

Teachers are responsible for how learning is organized and processed. Connected structure pushes children toward healthy activities, thoughts, and emotional pay-offs. A common simplistic use of organizational structure is how a teacher designs a seating plan. Children organized in rows facing the front of the classroom are being encouraged to work independently in a teacher-centered learning structure. A teacher pursuing a cooperative student-centered learning experience will be better off arranging seating in a circle or in groups.

Authentic structure sets the parameters for authentic learning process. Competitive versus cooperative structures is a good example. If a unit or lesson culminates with a high-stakes test, the push is toward extrinsic motivators and stressful emotions. A unit wrapped in the Six Ps and formative assessments is far less stressful and pushes children toward authentic attachments. For highly connected children, competitive structures can be an exhilarating authentic exercise because they possess healthy perspectives that make the return to emotional balance easy. For the disconnected, it is always a distressing distraction.

Testing and Assessment Strategies

Support in competitive environments is illogical. If you fail, I win. If I bully you, I am stronger. If I score higher on a test, my status trumps yours. There is far less motivation to support others with a belief system and school structure based on competition and status. A shift of thinking from competitive to cooperative structures and environments is necessary.

Dialing back a dependence on classroom structures and educational processes linked to competition and curricular testing leaves room for activities and outcomes grounded in connection skills, contribution, cooperation, and collective safety. If lessons align with these objectives, children will notice that connection matters to their teacher and perhaps it should matter to them. Once they experience authentic payoffs associated with cooperative tasks and environments, proof of a viable rewarding alternative emerges.

Testing and competition do not have to be dirty words if their purpose is authentically aligned with learning, emotional growth, and resiliency. Teachers who begin with an authentic perspective of why they are testing and what it is they hope to achieve are in an advantageous position. Challenging traditional testing objectives is a significant step toward reducing student anxiety. When testing shifts toward growth objectives rather than ones of judgment, a believable story that connected learning matters more than grades unfolds. Summative testing does not have to be an anxious experience if packaged in connected thinking. It does not make sense to have a child walk away from a learning experience feeling bad. If the desired outcome is healthy emotional attachment outcomes, the structures, perspectives, and methodologies of testing should reflect this.

Performance or summative testing is typically quite stressful, and the contribution toward learning is questionable. When deadlines and final judgment are thrown into the mix, even the tasks designed to allow freedom and creative expression of learning are accompanied by a significant increase in pressure that ultimately stifles the performance and creative thought teachers may hope to see (Amabile, 1996). A move toward formative evaluation is a good step to reduce anxiety levels. It aligns better with connected learning experiences and eliminates the arbitrary finality out of learning assessment. Project-based evaluations, concept maps, presentations, self-evaluations, portfolios, observations, or simple discussions are examples of stress reducing, assessment strategies.

One of the troubles with traditional testing is its reputation as an unpleasant experience. Students can question why they feel this way. If they take the time to think about the irrational response a shift in perspective becomes possible. A sheet of paper with questions is stressful only because a student's belief tells him it is. Teachers can help with the shift by rewriting the rules of assessment. Expressing summative testing as a measure of growth rather than a finite measure of judgment is a good start.

Another way to promote a mindset where testing is not just about marks is with the introduction of the cooperative test. The purpose of a cooperative test is to work together on a common goal with contribution, effort, and healthy attachments driving the learning process. Help or graciously accept help. Practice supportive language, coaching skills, or share thoughts of appreciation. The competitive reputation of testing becomes a sideshow rather than the main feature.

FIGURE 8.1

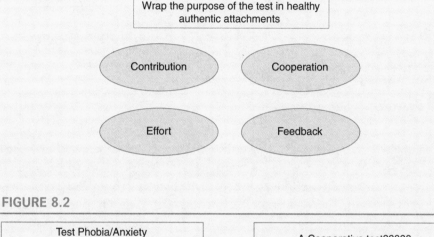

Wrap the purpose of the test in healthy authentic attachments

Contribution

Cooperation

Effort

Feedback

FIGURE 8.2

Test Phobia/Anxiety
(Fear of failure, "less than")

A Cooperative test?????

Product-Focused Test reinforces
unhealthy payoffs

Process-Oriented Examination
reinforces healthy attachments

IMAGE SOURCES: iStock.com/wdnet (*left*), iStock.com/steve debenport (*right*)

Guided reflection or self-assessment can measure feelings and healthy attachments linked to the examination process. Dial back the competitive reputation of testing further by encouraging celebrations of a communal score and improvement by any individual or the group as a whole. Healthy emotional payoffs belong to all rather than only the elite few. Processing test scores in healthy ways can be part of an authentic learning process. If students are unsatisfied with the outcome, get help and continue until they are satisfied. If the experience has left them feeling emotionally distressed, they should reflect on why and think of ways to support each other. No pressure or judgment, just relaxed, authentic learning and feedback.

FIGURE 8.3

Imagine If:

After preparing with a cooperative test, Karen scores her best ever: 8/10.

"Susie was great—she really helped me a lot! I think I can do this."

Healthy endorphins, payoffs, and attachments in action.

You can tell that grade-obsessed Susie made a real difference in somebody's life.

"How do you feel about that?"

"Karen is so happy—and that makes me feel awesome!"

IMAGE SOURCE: iStock.com/stevendevenport

The complete elimination of testing will probably never happen, and perhaps it should not because it comes with a potential upside. Competition and judgment of work by others is a reality children will face in life and work beyond the classroom. Competitive testing is practice for processing this type of inevitable challenge, and as such, it is an opportunity to nurture healthy attachments and resiliency. Emotional preparation needs to be part of the testing structure to make that happen. Studying harder is not the challenge for a healthy productive outcome and attachment. It is perspective.

Mr. Stevens

Testing and the Bad Wolf

Today during your test, the Bad Wolf may pay you a visit. He will come with a sinister plan. He wants you to feel unnecessarily stressed. He knows this will make it difficult to think clearly. He wants you to fail and feel less smart than you are. This is how he feeds himself.

It is normal to feel a little nervous during a test, but if your thoughts and emotions begin to get away from you, know the Bad Wolf is up to his tricks. Acknowledge his presence, and choose not to play his game. Breathe, relax, and do your best. Your worries will pass. Before we start our test, let's take a moment to shake out the nerves and put your Good Wolf in charge.

Here are a few strategies Mr. Stevens could use to help students feed their Good Wolf.

- *Breathing*

  - *Breathe in through your nose for four counts.*

  - *Hold it for three counts.*

  - *Slowly breathe out for four counts.*

  - *Hold for three counts.*

  - *Repeat.*

- *Mental Vacation*

  - *Close your eyes.*

  - *Go to your happy place where you feel calm and safe. Go to the beach, the forest, sit with your favorite book, or hold hands with your best friend.*

  - *Paint a vivid picture. What are you experiencing through your feelings and senses? What do you feel, see, hear, or smell?*

  - *Breathe slowly, and allow yourself to relax in your happy place.*

- *Active Strategies*

  - *Talk it through with a friend. Share good energy and maybe a laugh.*

  - *Exercise. Go for a walk or a jog. Share a stretch.*

  - *Trigger word. When you begin to drift, use your trigger word to remind yourself it is time to return to the truth of the present moment. Literally, shake off the nerves. Jell-O, Jell-O, Jell-O.*

  - *Listen to soothing music*

Pro-tip: There are many helpful anxiety apps that offer good strategies.

Lesson Title: <u>**Trinomial Factoring Test**</u>   *Date* _____

Connection Intention: <u>Relaxation, emotional awareness, connection with</u>
<u>personal truth, and a healthy perspective of testing. Starve the Bad Wolf!</u>

Prescribed Learning Outcome(s): <u>Demonstrate trinomial factoring competencies.</u>

The truth is that a test is just a test and life will go on regardless of the score. It will not dictate the authentic truth of a child unless unhealthy emotions, beliefs, and attachments dictate the outcome. Teachers can help students perform better with mindfulness and relaxation techniques. They can also remind their students that effort is always worthy of celebration and a score is just a number.

THE ROLE OF STRUCTURE

An anxiety intervention is dependent on a stable, consistent, safe environment. Close is not good enough, and this responsibility loosely handed to children lacking the skills or desire to embrace a connected culture of safety and support is dangerous. This necessitates a high degree of teacher interaction and predictable structure that sets a baseline for activities, behaviors, and safety. Authentic structure is not a set of rules to manage disconnecting behaviors. It is a comprehensive framework pushing students toward healthy experiences, emotional rewards, and beliefs.

Connected children do not need rules to guide them toward authentic learning and reward; authentic beliefs and attachments do that for them. Disconnected children lack a similar guidance system. Those suffering from emotional addiction and unhealthy attachments experience pressures that send them in the opposite direction. Structure sets the daily parameters that help keep them on track until healthy connections and attachments emerge and take over. Consistency helps children relax, prepare for, and anticipate learning challenges. Its predictability reduces anxiety, nurtures healthy thought patterns, and creates the support that increases the probability of healthy attachment outcomes.

Structure of any type may seem to contradict the natural free play learning environments that worked so well for hunter-gatherer children. In theory, free play learning structures should work equally well in today's world, but there are many factors working against it. The first is the stifling nature of existing educational models that undervalue and limit opportunities for play. An even greater consideration may be that anxious children with weak connection skills often do not know how to play or socialize. A playful state of mind is learning process at its best, but structure that helps children rebalance and acquire connection skills first is a responsible consideration.

Authentic connected learning begins with safe relaxed environments and daily connection intentions. It ends with healthy emotional payoffs and attachments. Authentic structure is everything in between that makes it consistently happen. Routines for healthy thinking patterns, relaxation, practicing connection skills, and learning how to get the most out of connected moments create immersive experiences. Structure facilitates a connected, reliable learning experience accepted as the norm even when a bad day, unhealthy emotional attachments, or the addictive drive make a showing.

Authentic structures make avoidance of connection a less viable option. This is a significant objective because the disconnected will avoid uncomfortable short-term connection initiatives believing they will soon go away. The pattern of behavior below represents what connected people do naturally in their daily lives. In addiction interventions, the imposed parameters are a necessary lifeline to stay connected with daily intentions and healthy emotional payoffs. The Lesson Plan Template in the following chapter is remarkably similar.

A Five-Step Daily Structure for Connectedness and Happiness

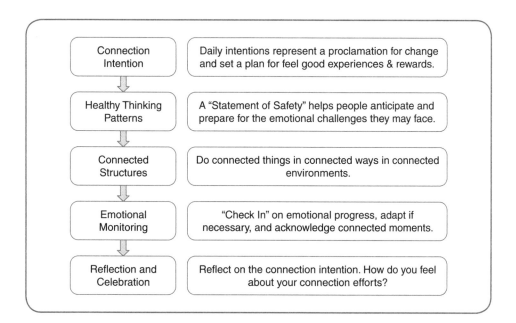

The connected objective of high structure is to make it redundant and unnecessary. It is there to ensure safety in the short term and nudge children toward authentic attachments and beliefs that make teacher control or intervention unnecessary in

FIGURE 8.4

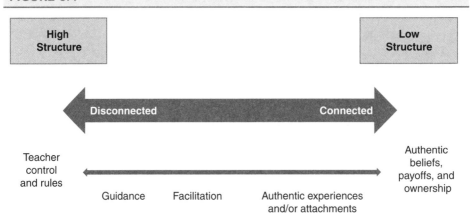

the future. Herein lies a potential contradiction. Imposed rules and implicit directions take control away from children, which has a tendency to exacerbate feelings of anxiety. It takes time to nurture the skills and connected beliefs to empower children to make good choices, but the long-term goal remains: choices guided by authentic belief and authentic motivators.

Structure and connection objectives should never disappear, but the degree to which they control what children do should. The most powerful healthy attachments form when children own what they do. Teachers and school rules will not be there to make decisions for students when they graduate. Young adults need to rely on healthy attachments and belief systems to do that.

Another factor teachers need to consider is the level of challenge and the emotional readiness of children. The stress response triggered by the learning experience needs to align with the children's ability to cope with their emotions and the degree to which they effectively and safely support each other. Structure is one way teachers control and manage this delicate balance of skill sets and challenge.

DYNAMIC STRUCTURE

Connected children possess the healthy attachments that make them feel secure, valued, and resilient. They also find great reward in supporting those around them. In this scenario, there is less need for overt teacher supervision. It is time for teachers to let go and allow the connected beliefs and attachments they have nurtured to take over and allow children to soar.

There is also the reality that even the most connected children will fall out of balance, and shifting structures to meet the emotional needs of the moment may be necessary. Teachers are ultimately in charge of safety and learning standards and should never really give away control. They will always be responsible for discreetly gauging anxiety levels and creating structure that is appropriate.

Sometimes structure and activities are not about learning content at all. The sole purpose may be lowering anxiety or preparing students for upcoming challenges. In other scenarios, teachers may feel comfortable trusting free play, challenge, and self-discovery as the optimal organization for learning. When appropriate, setting aside precious time to naturally establish their own boundaries and become accountable for learning, healthy relationships, and relaxed feelings is always a worthy investment. Such activities could include:

- Free play, natural learning, and discovery

- Passionately pursue an interest

- Exercise, yoga, meditation, or mindfulness

- Study in nature

- Social connections

Ms. Grabowski

Why Fight Nature?

The science review was going poorly. The work was not particularly challenging, but she sensed feelings of anxiety in her classroom. Perhaps they were worried about the test tomorrow. Children bored by the task were disturbing others who were trying to read and answer questions. When Johnny got bored that could be a very bad thing, but today he was simply staring out the window, not disturbing anyone. Ms. G thought about leaving it alone, just let the sleeping dogs lie, but instead she went and sat beside the boy and stared out the window alongside him. It was a beautiful day. She turned to Johnny,

"You're right; we should go outside."

She paired up the students, and out they went.

"Take a moment to search out the most comfortable spot and enjoy studying together. All I ask in return is to remember your friend has an upcoming test. You are capable. Prepare each other, and perhaps tomorrow you will have something to celebrate together."

What If?

Two of Ms. G's students do not embrace the support and relaxation intention for test preparation. What should she do if

- They didn't understand the intention: **Clarify and reiterate**

- Attachments to purpose and support are weak: **Increase structure**, partner them up with more connected students

- They are emotionally out of balance and the test is not that important to them at the moment: **Consider another strategy**. Maybe they need a walk before getting down to business. Remember, addiction loves imposed control and a good fight. Big unhealthy payoffs await

- **Always think emotional reward** when trying to steer behavior

- **Celebrate!** Make a big deal out of the healthy energy the vast majority of the class is embracing. You are on the right track with an effective intention

Authentic or connected structure can offer short-term safety and stability in anxious environments where unhealthy attachments thrive and fight for control. It also enables children to explore and control their own destiny when they are ready to do so. The dynamic rules of authentic structure always have purpose and help keep children on the connected pathway. In the next chapter, we turn talk into daily action with a teacher's most basic tool for structure: the lesson plan. Consistent structure helps teachers and students stay the course, especially when things get difficult.

Johnny Meets Inubu

The new kid looked different, dressed strangely, and had an unusual accent that was difficult to understand, but what caught Johnny's interest were his eager eyes and the biggest smile he had ever seen. This was unexpected from a kid who had things so bad. At the end of class he cautiously introduced himself and began their trek around the school. Usually Johnny felt uncomfortable meeting new people. He always felt like he was being judged, but he didn't get that vibe from Inubu at all.

Things went really well. His new classmate enthusiastically listened to everything he had to say about his school. Johnny was having fun and didn't want to damage the mood so he thought it would be best if he kept his own school experiences to himself.

As the days went by the pair spent a lot of time together at school. Ms. Grabowski partnered them up on a green waste recycling project that had to be presented in 2 weeks. Inubu was smart, but the research was difficult for him. He had never used a computer before. Johnny did most of the work, but Inubu's enthusiasm made it fun.

It had been a long time since Johnny asked a friend to come to his house and hang out. As they passed through a park on the way to his home Johnny couldn't help but notice Inubu's interest in the trees.

"These trees are not like our own. Are they difficult to climb?"

Before Johnny had time to think about it, he was higher than he had ever been. It was pretty scary, but his climbing mate skillfully helped him through the trickier parts. He found a comfortable branch to sit on, took a breath of fresh air, enjoyed the view, and couldn't help but make a note of how relaxed he felt. There the boys sat as Inubu shared the story of his life in vivid detail. The tale was sad but also amazing. The boy had shared his father's last words with him. Johnny felt very special.

"I need to study hard in memory of my father. I want to make a better life for my brother and mother."

Maybe the world was good. Maybe Johnny could make a difference, too.

They finished the day having fun working on their project back at Johnny's place. On his way out the door his new friend turned toward Johnny, shared his remarkable smile, and nodded his head.

"Respect." And he walked out the door.

That was an unusual way to say goodbye. It felt like a farewell, compliment, and a thank-you all wrapped up into one. Inubu was a friend, a real friend, and it felt really good. In fact, Johnny couldn't remember the last time he felt this way. He sat down on the couch next to his brother and went to grab his game controller when a thought passed his mind. They weren't very close, and a significant amount of his energy was usually spent resenting his brother's successes, but he paused and thought for a moment, Why not?

"Do you feel like going to the park and throwing the ball?"

"Sure. Sounds good."

The boys strolled through the kitchen to grab a freshly baked cookie. They smiled at their mother on their way out the door.

Today, tears of a different kind fell across her face.

CHAPTER 9

The Lesson and Unit Plan

The lesson plan is the focal point of every teacher-training program and is the organizational tool that practicing teachers use to map out their creative teaching strategies. It represents the standard for good teaching practices. Templates are remarkably similar, regardless of the training program that initiates the career of all teachers. Form follows purpose. The purpose of traditional lesson plan design is delivery of curriculum. The Emotionally Connected Classroom lesson plan is different. The objective is connectedness, emotional alignment, and nurturing healthy brains for inspired, lifelong learning and happiness long after the classroom doors close. It is designed to feed the Good Wolf and starve the Bad Wolf during and after the learning experience.

> *"Education is what remains after one has forgotten what one has learned in school."*
> Albert Einstein

Modern progressive curriculums leave room for teachers to put more energy into the long-term benefits of socioemotional competencies, healthy thinking, and emotional wellness. However, when teachers in training settle in to create lessons on a typical template, there is very little directional push toward healthy emotional learning experiences. It is almost a certainty that references to lasting emotional and belief attachments are not on the page. The assumption is that young teachers will figure that part out on their own. This glaring miss of design is a confusing matter for young teachers wanting to make a true impact in the daily lives and futures of their students. From start to finish, the Emotionally Connected lesson template prioritizes an authentic emotional experience and arms teachers with the necessary tools to target healthy payoffs and quickly move with the dynamic mood and needs of their classroom.

The Emotionally Connected Classroom Lesson Plan Template

Lesson Title _____ **Date** _____

- **Connection Intention(s) (Six Ps)**: A specific and measurable feeling, belief, or behavior (e.g., What do bravery, support, or healthy thinking look like?).

- **Prescribed Learning Outcome(s)**: Content-based outcomes are linked to authentic connections and healthy, emotional payoffs for inspired learning.

Healthy Attachment Strategy (at least one should be used every lesson)

1. **Everyday healthy connections: Connection skills, people, purpose, play, passion**

2. **Healthy thinking patterns: Mindfulness and connections with authentic truth (Statement of Safety)**

3. **Challenge, resiliency, and growth: Stressful learning challenge, support, and emotional balance**

LESSON	NOTES	TIME
Introduction: **Anticipatory Set:** Create interest and gauge current understanding of the curricular topic. **Statement of Safety:** A statement, story, or activity that builds a sense of safety, team, and present moment awareness intended to reduce anxiety and prepare students for the challenge ahead. A promise of feel-good payoffs reinforces the intention objective and sets the emotional stage for the challenge ahead.		
Main Activity and Lesson Structure: Use connection intentions to drive the lesson, achieve curricular objectives, and nurture healthy attachments. Structure should reflect the emotional readiness of students, encourage connections, and limit avoidance. The task, challenge, coping strategies, and connection objectives must be specific and clear. **Checking In:** What opportunities will students have to check in on their feelings and performance? How will connection objectives be measured and refined? **Stamping Behaviors:** How will authentic behaviors and feelings be stamped? Nurture connections linking authentic behaviors, thoughts, and healthy emotional payoffs. Celebrate and elevate **WOW!** moments worthy of remembering.		
Connection Assessment and Reflection (measure and celebrate attachment outcomes): Self-assessment, reflection, and celebration. How do you feel about your efforts? Has a healthy belief of feeling been nurtured?		
Closure: How will the lesson be closed? Review activity, reinforce connection objective. Link to new lesson.		

Teacher Reflection: How do you feel about the connections that were made during the lesson? How could you improve on the quality of connections next time? _____

LESSON INTENTIONS AND ATTACHMENT STRATEGIES

"We teach students, not curriculum." There is no need to demonize content-based curriculum. It is important and necessary. In its own right, much of it is engaging and interesting and comes with its own authentic rewards. After all, we became art teachers, math teachers, music teachers, or science teachers because we thought the subject matter was fun and rewarding. Nonetheless, relying on curricular content alone for inspiration falls short, especially for the disconnected. A concerted effort to wrap curriculum in healthy connections and emotional payoffs is necessary.

An effective lesson plan begins with a clearly defined purpose. Is it curricular or is it connection based? Hopefully, it is both. Teachers can use the Six Ps' intention and attachment strategies to infuse inspiration and healthy emotions for a memorable curricular experience. Sure, repetition may have laid down some well-worn neural pathways to remember content, but the vast majority of real learning memories exist because of a link to the emotional part of educational experiences.

Ms. Grabowski and the Go Green Project

Be Supportive and Brave!

Connection Intention(s): *Be a great Supporter.* Use healthy emotional energy and language to reduce anxiety of presenters *Be Brave.* Graciously embrace support, be mindful, and practice telling your story with reckless enthusiasm. Mistakes are okay!

Curricular Objective: Demonstrate an understanding of green environmental alternatives, issues, and solutions through PowerPoint presentations.

Susan was pleased with the hard work her students put into the green environment projects. There was much to celebrate already, but many remained nervous about the presentations. What a great opportunity to learn to be brave. Wrapping the presentation in healthy thoughts and intentions was probably a good place to start. She wanted the projects remembered for the right reasons. Support and enthusiasm always feels good. It makes bravery a little easier.

"Today we will face a challenge, but we will feed the Good Wolf."

Ms. Grabowski used all three of the Six Ps' attachment strategies to support her connection intentions. Sharing healthy energy is a great way to demonstrate support and trigger healthy endorphin payoffs. Smiles and laughter are contagious and reduce anxious feelings. Accepting support is a healthy thinking pattern. It mitigates feelings of judgment that may otherwise dominate the experience. Stay grounded and own your emotions. The presentation is an example of a challenge students can use to grow, build resiliency, and celebrate efforts together.

THE INTRODUCTION

The introduction is an opportunity to create interest and link prior learning to the upcoming lesson. Its primary function is nurturing healthy thinking patterns and mindsets to prepare children for the learning experience or task ahead. It consists of two parts: the Anticipatory Set and the Statement of Safety.

Anticipatory Set. The Anticipatory Set is an opportunity to create excitement about the day's activities. Investing time that clearly explains the curricular objectives goes a long way to alleviate anxious responses that may occur during the lesson. The Anticipatory Set also recalls previous learning and connection successes relevant to the current lesson to begin the story of competence and believable safety.

Statement of Safety. Learning is supposed to feel good. The Statement of Safety is an opportunity for the teacher to introduce a story or activity that builds a sense of safety and emotional excitement about the connection task ahead. A promise of feel-good payoffs reinforces the connection intention and sets a hopeful positive emotional tone for the learning task ahead. The Statement of Safety gives children the emotional tools to get the most out of the Six Ps' attachment experience. It is also a great time to proclaim or promise a collective intent to share healthy energy, support, and protect each other.

When the connection intention of the day falls into the category of less threatening, everyday healthy connections, a relaxed story of peace, and a promise that smiles, laughing, and working together that will make their learning a more pleasurable endeavor may be in order. Relax, embrace healthy connections, and be prepared to reflect on and celebrate the small, feel-good moments to come.

If the attachment strategy relates to healthy thinking patterns, the story turns to mindfulness and present thinking strategies. Students are competent, authentic support is everywhere, challenge is good, and at the end of the day, everything will be okay. This is a truthful story children can use to stay grounded in the present moment when anxiety tries to take them away. Nurturing healthy thinking patterns plays an important role in hedging the bet on an authentic attachment outcome. This may include mindfulness strategies like "I See You," positive self-talk, relaxed breathing, emotional awareness, or checking in with present moment awareness. The more vivid the story of truth and safety, the more emotionally prepared and resilient children will be for challenges during the lesson.

If the lesson ahead involves a significant emotional challenge, it is time to pull connected skill sets together. Challenge is difficult, and it will be uncomfortable. It is best to be truthful and honest about it. Discomfort is part of the process, and avoidance is not an option. It is going to happen so the authentic choice is using it advantageously for a positive rewarding outcome. Emotional preparation and anticipation reduces anxiety and can help children avoid the shock of being caught off guard and unarmed. The value of challenge is not usually an attractive draw for anxious children. Believable, connected support and healthy thinking patterns are a great way to be begin the statement of safety. A compelling story and prospect of an "imagine if" or "Wow!" moment can help even the most anxious child get excited about challenge. Wanting or looking forward to challenge is the death knell for unnecessary anxiety.

Ms. Grabowski

Driving Out the Fear

The class was feverously working to get their facts just right and packing in as much information as possible. She hoped for something much different. A fearless, passionate story shared with fun and enthusiasm was what she envisioned, but it certainly was not what the children were practicing. It was time to regroup and clarify her connection intention and statement of safety.

"I want to take a moment and remind you of the point of the presentation. Going green is about caring, and a fearless, passionate story is how you will prove that it matters. If this sounds scary, do not worry, your classmates will celebrate your bravery and commitment toward your message, mistakes and all. Your classmates will remember your emotion and passion, not facts. The anxiety you may feel is unnecessary and gets in the way of having fun. Let it go, and a greater truth will reveal itself. Bravery is liberating and feels amazing. I promise you, it will be okay. Your connection task today is to be a supportive coach. When practicing, set high standards, celebrate and laugh at the big mistakes, be loud and proud, and remind your teammate that enthusiastic effort is a no fail endeavor. Help your partner feel really great about being brave."

The noise that followed was far greater than expected. Susan was a little distressed about disturbing the class across the hall but when she saw Johnny and Inubu dancing and chanting to an African tribal song, she pushed the feeling away and joined in. The noise was a tangible measure of authentic connection she could live with.

BODY AND STRUCTURE

This part of the lesson plan describes the environments we choose, how children are organized, and the teaching strategies used. Strategies are always student centered and attempt to create conditions enabling children to freely exchange energy, share ideas, move, create, celebrate and explore. Sitting in rows with little opportunity to express feelings during or after a learning experience is a definite miss in this regard.

 TRY THIS!

Partners in Mathematics: Power of 3

- Each group will consist of three members; consider yourself a team. Working alone is not an option.
- During lecture, one partner will take notes; the others will focus on understanding the lesson.
- After the lesson, students will share the notes, check each other for understanding, and work together on the assigned exercises.
- Your efforts and input matter; help or graciously accept help.
- If your group is struggling, send one member to get help and return to share the solution.
- Use cooperative quizzes to prepare for unit examinations.
- Celebrate and reflect on your contributions.

 OR THIS!

Power of 7: Languages

Energy can fade when working on curricular tasks for longer periods. Children will invariably drift off task, and management may become a problem. Do not fight nature. There is an authentic need to be social. Embrace it, and use it to energize curricular tasks. Use a timer to limit curricular objectives to 7 minutes followed by 3 minutes of social time. Being firm on structured time will teach children to transition naturally between work and play. There may even be some urgency to stay on curricular tasks and get work done. Option: Students cannot use first language during social breaks. Have students come prepared with jokes to share.

Other classroom structures or strategies encourage movement, debate, or peer assessment. Teachers wearing their hunter-gatherer glasses see their class as a tribe in simpler times when connection with natural play, purpose, and teamwork were the norms for learning. They soon realize it isn't difficult to teach the same things in a different way. There is no need to reinvent the wheel, because countless tried and true connected structures already exist in classrooms.

Four Corners: Movement to demonstrate current understanding

Debate Circles: Listening to and expressing different perspectives

Two Stars and a Wish: Positive peer assessment skills

Think–Pair–Share: Cooperative summarization strategy

Jigsaw: Specialists move and share their expertise for a collective objective

Experiential Learning: Take a learning challenge into nature

Task Initiatives: Group problem solving builds connected culture

CONNECTION STANDARDS

Connected structure pushes children toward connected behaviors, but that doesn't necessarily mean they will be good at them. Good lessons and structure always begin with clear instructions and expectations, but connection standards can be a little trickier than the curricular ones teachers are used to demonstrating and assessing. Before learning activities begin, it is important to discuss or demonstrate standards for connection skills or thinking patterns to improve the quality of the connection objective and reiterate the point that learning process and a healthy emotional learning experience are the focus of the day. Clear standards and expectations are critically important for the intention assessment.

Modeling or demonstrating connected skills and actions provides tangible targets for connection intentions and sets standards for powerful connected moments. Tasks related to precise coaching, contribution, and use of positive language are easy to target and assess. Teaching children to express their feelings in a physical way with bigger smiles, eye contact, energetic gestures, or loud laughter serve as good indicators of connected moments. They also dial up the emotional response. Connected actions backed-up with free-flowing, healthy energy are measurable things and will always generously reward children with the endorphin payoffs teachers are shooting for.

Standards for beliefs and thinking patterns are somewhat trickier to manage. What does effort, healthy present thinking, authentic contribution, or bravery look like, and how do you measure it? Teachers are very intuitive when it comes to the authenticity of their students' efforts and beliefs, and if they look closely, they can probably guess when a connected moment has resulted in a healthy endorphin deposit. A warm look, a confident swagger, a celebrated response, or a gleeful, free-flowing laugh all suggest a connected moment has occurred. These authentic gestures emote a healthy energy that says a great deal about the beliefs, feelings, and thinking patterns that accompanied the behavior or learning task. When students can make a similar connection, recognize their own emotions, and intuitively read the emotions of their peers, an understanding and standard for inspired, fearless learning is emerging.

A bold first step to challenge an unhealthy attachment or fear is a big deal. A healthy thought or belief may be difficult for children to assess early on. If a student does not know what bravery feels like, an "I think I was brave" assessment does not really mean much. Assessing a belief like bravery is easiest if expressed as a specific task or behavior. A student will challenge an unhealthy attachment, or they will not. Step in front of the volleyball even though you messed up last time. Take a deep breath, and project a loud voice when sharing a classroom answer. Share a warm hug or a compliment if it is something you do not normally do. As students get their bearings on what bravery, joy, or support feels like through doing, they will begin to have a benchmark for accurate connection assessment.

TRY THIS!

A common practice in the Emotionally Connected Classroom is sharing reflections or intention scores that represent how children feel about the connections intention experience. Sometimes a behavior, thought, or emotion experienced changes a belief system in some way, making life and learning a little bit better. Instead of giving a score, children can share their "WOW!" moment and celebrate with their classmates. Others will want a "WOW!" moment, too.

The gold standard of a connected moment is growth, change, and a measurable, authentic payoff, but that never happens without choice and commitment. The first step is always the hardest so it is important to acknowledge, assess, and celebrate authentic choice when it happens. Defining standards for authentic effort or engagement requires reflection on emotional experiences. "Big feelings" reflect high connection standards, regardless of the learning product or performance. It will be through real, emotionally charged experiences that students will learn what bravery or real contribution looks like.

CHECKING IN

Children can lose focus on connection objectives when they are used to judgment based on performance of curricular tasks. Teachers can stop activities at strategic moments throughout the lesson to refocus on the connection objective and check in with student progress and feelings. How children think they are doing is more important than how they think they did, because adjustments to emotional learning are most effective in the moment.

This type of formative assessment is often used to check for understanding of curricular objectives and maintain high standards during the learning process. Similar interjections can monitor emotions and thinking patterns. Checking in with feelings and beliefs helps children stay on track with emotional connection targets. Monitoring the emotional energy enables teachers to reset or adapt the intention when necessary. It also creates opportunities to celebrate magic, emotional moments.

 ## TRY THIS!

Fist to Five is a common formative assessment technique teacher's use to gauge current understanding of curricular concepts. It can also measure anxious feelings, feel-good payoffs, or commitment level to the connection intention.

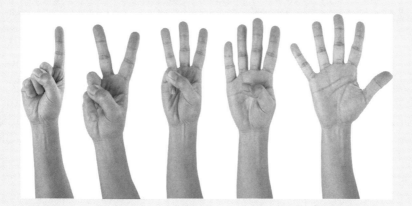

IMAGE SOURCE: iStock.com/bulentozber

During difficult challenges, students may experience unhealthy emotions that, left unchecked, can spiral to unmanageable levels and result in undesirable attachments. Emotional reflection allows children to regroup and practice strategies and healthy thinking patterns discussed in the Statement of Safety. Recognizing unnecessary, painful emotions and shifting toward healthy thought patterns can help students get back on track. Periodic time for reflection during lessons also allows students to practice their own intuitive senses that gauge the current emotional state of their peers and adjust their support strategies accordingly.

STAMPING BEHAVIORS

Consciously linking healthy emotions with behaviors and beliefs is an important part of the attachment process. This is something children do not always naturally do. It is quite possible that children will demonstrate connected behaviors and experience healthy endorphin-producing feelings during a lesson, but they may not recognize or take the time to process the cause and effect of the interaction. When a true-self moment happens, "Stamping Behaviors" can dial up the emotional experience for a more powerful attachment.

Sometimes it takes somebody else to point out the moment. Stamping Behaviors is particularly important for children crippled by self-doubt and unhealthy beliefs. A discreet whisper in the ear offering a congratulatory exclamation for contribution can trigger a personal reflection that changes the way children think about themselves. A more overt class-wide celebration of a special moment feels great and can set the connection benchmark for others to pursue. When healthy emotional experiences are powerful and linked to belief or behavior, the connection is indelibly "stamped" in the form of neurological change and lasting attachments. The behavior is hard-wired as desirable and becomes part of a connected mindset.

Teachers should always be on the lookout for the special moments that may go unnoticed. A baby step in connection may require a significant moment of bravery, and the opportunity to nurture a healthy attachment may not come again soon. Of course, teachers cannot be there for all moments, so a better strategy is to foster a class of intuitive enthusiastic cheerleaders who encourage and hunt for authentic moments to stamp. When children are being brave and taking risk, they like to know that somebody is watching and willing to support and celebrate their bravery. They like to be caught winning the authentic game. The ones who notice and celebrate the little connection victories of others become popular in the most authentic ways.

LESSON ASSESSMENT, REFLECTION, AND CLOSURE

A connection objective identified at the start of lesson that is not measured in some way leaves the impression that it was not that important in the first place. This scenario also leaves children not knowing if they have achieved their connection goals. Summative, product-based assessments and testing do not align well with connected experiences. Complex rubrics measuring behaviors attempt to offer authentic assessment, but they are often confusing. By the time scoring calculations from all the boxes are complete, meaningless and inaccurate assessments may be all that remains.

Formative self-assessment is the natural response to connection objectives that are both subjective and dynamic and belong to no one but the student. What happens if a student is not good at self-reflection and incapable of accuracy? The misleading stories that accompany emotional addictions, anxiety, and unhealthy attachments may make it seem impossible for students to be honest or truthful when they adamantly believe their story to be true.

Another problem arises with grade-obsessed students. Reflections linked to percentages or a traditional marking scheme are a challenge for this type of disconnection. Will parents be getting an accurate authentic account of how their child is doing? Under these conditions, it is understandably difficult for teachers to give control and responsibility for assessment to students. Developing skill sets for accurately assessing connection objectives and emotions is an important part of preparing children for a connected life beyond the classroom. There will be no teacher by their side to tell them how they are doing as they move on to the next stage of their life. It will take practice, and a great deal of guidance.

Children new to reflecting on connection objectives will often drift a considerable distance from authentic truth. This is an expected condition of inexperience. It is not the teachers' role to be the judge validating or refuting the assessment of a student's beliefs or feelings, but they should use their own experience and intuition to help push students on their journey and quest for authentic truth.

Effectively processing beliefs and emotions demands truth. If children are off the mark, they need to know. Assessment that falls below actual performance benefits from guided reflection and questioning that bring the child closer to truth. When the self-assessment is unrealistically positive, some teachers struggle if they obsess about upsetting their student or feel they may be impeding on a child's right to own their self-assessment. Teachers letting this learning moment slide are allowing false beliefs to fester and grow. This is neither kind nor compassionate. It is not an insult for a teacher to tell a student, "I think you have more to give." It is a compliment. "You are greater than you believe, and I will help you get there!" Honesty is always more palatable if it is wrapped in authentic, positive energy and a promise of support and something better. The ultimate purpose of the lesson closure is to have children feel good about their daily experience and hopeful of a better, truthful future. They will have learned facts, knowledge, and skills, but in some way, they are leaving the classroom more connected, and that is something worth celebrating. Consider closure the knockout punch for false-self beliefs.

One way to increase reflection accuracy is for students to share their thoughts with their peers. With practice and guidance, children can translate connections and feelings into simple rubrics or numerical scores that measure an authentic learning experience with remarkable accuracy and consistency. Sharing thoughts or scores is one more way to celebrate connected moments that may set benchmarks for others to pursue. "I want to feel that way, too." Discussing why a score may be too high or too low allows the class to refine their own ability to assess accurately. At any time, classmates can opt in and share the ways their peer performed or made their own day a little better.

THE UNIT PLAN: A SET OF INTENTIONS

It is possible for a belief or mindset to experience significant change in response to a singular intention or lesson experience, but it is more common for the process of influencing a personal belief or connection skill set to take time. This is especially true for intentions attempting to rewire chronic, unhealthy thoughts or behaviors. Setting intentions in the form of a unit plan has several advantages over a single lesson format because

- Complex intentions take time to understand and embrace

- Time exists to develop connection skills that support big idea intentions

- Different units or subject areas offer unique, in-depth opportunities to nurture meaningful connections

Indian Horse: Unit Plan Case Study

The Shakespeare unit went very well, and Ms. Watt wanted to build on the evolving connections and personal growth in her classroom. *Indian Horse* is a novel exposing a dark and painful chapter in Canadian history. The Canadian government forcibly ripped indigenous youth from their families and placed them in residential schools run by the Catholic Church. Residential schools operated on the false premise that eradication of First Nation culture and traditional ways of life would give the children a better shot at fitting into Canadian society. The process was painful and often abusive. It was a defining example of the destructive power of disconnection. An experiment on a grand scale gone wrong demonstrated what happens when people are forced to be something they are not. Many years after the residential schools shut their doors, the devastating scope of cultural trauma remains. Ms. Watt wanted to do the subject justice. An opportunity existed within the tragic story to examine and value the importance of cultural connectedness and personal truth. She thought about what *Indian Horse* had to offer and then planned her unit as a set of intentions.

POTENTIAL BIG IDEA INTENTIONS

- **Examine the Connection–Disconnection theme:** *Indian Horse* is a literal expression of disconnection and the emotional survival mode response it creates. In the absence of healthy connections, unhealthy connections become more attractive.

- **Learn to process guilt, shame, and regret in healthy ways:** Resiliency begins with letting go of unhealthy emotions. In the context of this story, it is about forgiveness and acceptance of truth.

- **Celebrate First Nation culture as an excellent example of connected lifestyle and thinking:** Connections to nature, the land, art, cultural stories, learning, sharing, and the concept of tribe are best-case examples of connected culture aligned with natural authentic emotional payoffs. Western culture could learn something!

- **Contribute to the cause:** Create a project that positively contributes to the reconciliation effort or First Nation culture.

NOTE. A traditional content learning strategy would look at these intentions as questions to be answered in some way and then assessed as a grade. A connection approach looks at these intentions as a potential authentically rewarding emotional experience. Feed the Good Wolf.

Embracing these lofty intentions was a significant task for a class still developing basic connection and communication skills. Ms. Watt realized her class still needed to work on lower level connection skills that would support the Big Idea intentions. Again, she thought about ways to infuse the Six Ps to mitigate emotional roadblocks and add motivation to her daily lessons.

POTENTIAL CONNECTION INTENTIONS (SIX Ps) TO SUPPORT THE BIG IDEAS

- **Value yourself:** Share ideas, practice communication skills. It feels good to contribute ideas!

- **Be brave, take risk:** Dive in and share your thoughts. Trust that your peers will support you. There is no right or wrong with opinion.

- **Be prepared and deliberate:** Organize ideas into succinct thoughts.

- **Value others:** Listening skills, collective objectives, seek out and value the ideas of others. Everybody likes a good listener who appreciates the thoughts of others!

- **Share healthy energy:** Attract the attention you deserve, and provide the attention you would want.

- **Celebrate cultural differences:** Value cultural differences; they are interesting and help us grow. Understanding unites us.

- **True self exercises:** Strengthen connections with your authentic self.

- **Be emotionally accessible and vulnerable:** Walk in the shoes of another, and understand the feelings of others.

Ms. Watt was happy with the ideas generated, but she was concerned that too many connection targets might spread time thin and limit the emotional response she hoped to elicit. The less is more principle made sense. While she was quite certain she would touch on all the intentions, she paired the list down to a manageable list she felt would be useful for setting daily targets.

INDIAN HORSE (MADISON WATT)

Connection Intention: Examine the Connection–Disconnection theme. *Indian Horse* is a literal expression of cultural disconnection and the emotional survival mode response it creates. Understand First Nation challenges from the perspective of forced disconnection.

Supporting Connection Intentions

- **Be emotionally accessible and vulnerable:** Walk in the shoes of another and understand the feelings of others.

- **Value others:** Practice communication skills, and value the ideas of others. Everybody likes a good listener!

- **Share healthy energy:** Attract the attention you deserve, and provide the attention you would want.

- **Celebrate cultural differences:** Value cultural differences; they are interesting and help us grow. Understanding unites us.

(For more sample unit plan intentions, see pages 185–187.)

During her Indian Horse *unit, Ms. Watt selected connection intentions to guide and infuse healthy energy into her daily lesson plans. Valuing others and listening skills were intentions she used for several lessons. At the close of each class, she took a few minutes to collect reflections that scored how students felt they did with their connection intention. Everybody likes a good listener, supportive partner, or enthusiastic participant. During reflection, students often spoke up to celebrate their classmates' efforts.*

IMAGE SOURCE: Courtesy of Madison Watt

WHAT IF THINGS STILL GO WRONG?

Teachers expect that things will not always go as planned. Well-thought-out lessons or unit plans come with no guarantee children will respond positively. On any given day a student may get caught up in unhealthy thinking patterns, experience anxious emotions, or underachieve in terms of curricular objectives or connection targets, but that isn't really a problem with honest reflection and a plan to persevere or move on. Bad days and failures are a natural part of learning and building resiliency. If unhealthy behaviors and emotions are chronic, then that is another matter altogether.

Even in the most connected environments, emotional addictions will do all they can to ensure their host will share their pain and feed off the feelings of distress they create in lives of those around them. Teachers and classmates who understand the workings of emotional addictions are prepared to protect themselves and starve the addiction. Together they are prepared to nurture a believable true-self story for those who need it most.

Johnny and Inubu

The Recycling Presentation

Johnny and Inubu worked really hard together, and Johnny actually felt pretty prepared, but it didn't change the fact he always hated presentations. He was so nervous the last time that he froze and couldn't remember anything. Classroom laughter sent him over the top. It didn't end well for him. He was anxious for other reasons now. Things were going better, and he didn't want to ruin it.

When it was their turn to go, they walked to the front of the class together. Inubu turned to his friend and gave him an enthusiastic high five, a firm handshake, and a confident nod of the head. He spoke his now-trademarked words.

"Respect. We got this!"

Johnny laughed, and his nerves receded. Inubu didn't know as much as Johnny, but he started things off with a passionate and richly described story about recycling in a country where you don't really own much. Johnny was so proud of his seemingly fearless friend. He made Johnny feel just a little bit braver.

He had a tough time matching the energy that seemed to come out of Inubu so freely, but he did his best as he worked his way through the majority of the presentation. He even managed to throw in a composting fart joke the class greeted with animated laughter. Johnny was happy at school like never before. As their presentation came to a close, an enthusiastic celebration for their entertaining performance erupted. Ms. G always encouraged the class to clap, but this felt unusually special. Inubu embraced Johnny in an uncomfortably weird but wonderful hug. His eyes watered, but he didn't really care. He couldn't wait to get home to tell his parents about his day.

It was the best day of teaching Susan ever had. This was truth revealed. Later that evening at home, she settled down with a glass of wine in her favorite chair. Her smile had not diminished.

CHAPTER 10

Control, Drama, and Choice

Throwing anxious emotions at dysfunctional behaviors in the classroom is nothing more than fuel for the addictive fire. When teachers step back from drama and look at their own emotional energy, addictive tendencies, or emotional triggers, a new perspective and potential for meaningful change and healing reveals itself.

Authentic connections are easier when things are good, or at the very least, headed in a better direction. When survival mode and dysfunction are at their worst, it can be extremely challenging. The exchange can throw those most willing to help into their own version of survival mode while they struggle to navigate the irrational and intense emotions thrown their way. There is nothing pleasant about it. This is also the time when connection with those we love is most important. Caring, patience, kindness, and understanding the nature of emotional battles can smooth out the bumps. The most painful moments often serve as the greatest opportunities for healing and healthy attachments as student's emotions settle and rebalance.

When teachers are overwhelmed and tired, they just want bad behaviors to go away. Quick fix management or control strategies are often the answer, but this is a slippery slope. As time and commitments to behavior management strategies grow, and fatigue inevitably sets in, putting off or ignoring less disruptive addictive behaviors until another time is a natural response. Allowing emotional addiction of any type or perceived severity to persist unchallenged results only in an unending and far more exhausting emotional experience for student and teacher alike. There is nothing easy about challenging unhealthy false-self attachments and emotional addictions. Things will always get worse before they get better.

Addiction is looking for an emotionally charged fight, and it wants to battle under terms that work in its favor. The arena of choice is emotional drama. Survival mode responses in the classroom can be incredibly disruptive. Other times they are hardly noticeable. Either way, if teachers are brave enough to address an emotional addiction, they can count on pushback and an escalation of unhealthy emotion and behaviors.

Rules, control, and even the best management strategies are short-term measures because the underlying drivers of the behavior remain. Teachers who do manage to control or eliminate unhealthy behaviors can be tricked by the illusion of short-term success, but the prospect of addictive behaviors emerging in another form that may be significantly more challenging is high. Control is the wrong target. In fact, it may be exactly what an emotionally imbalanced student pursues.

Control Dramas

Where our attention goes, our emotional energy follows. When we are balanced and relaxed, we freely share healthy positive energy with those around us. On the other hand, an out-of-balance person is always in a struggle to gain a sense of emotional control and is inclined to dominate others to gain it. Their compensatory strategy involves seeking out opportunities to steal energy from others and control them by any means possible (see Figure 10.1). If they are successful, a temporary high of power, security, and self-worth gives them a sense of control.

The strategy a person uses to garner control is dependent on the life experiences and attachments they live with. A bully persona or attachment may have emerged because of abuse at the hands of other intimidators. If students embrace this coping strategy as their own, they would run into problems if they tried to bully their own abuser, a teacher, or a larger kid, so they are naturally drawn toward individuals they feel are weaker and can be easily intimidated or frightened.

One would be naturally inclined to believe the victims of this exchange would do all they could to avoid this potentially frightening or dangerous scenario, but that is not necessarily the case. A student who has experienced a life of neglect and has been unable to count on others for protection may develop a "poor me" attachment and attempt to manipulate or control others through guilt or expectations of sympathy. The *Poor Me* is unconsciously drawn toward the *Intimidator* personality because the impending abuse will justify their expectation of shame from the bully or compassion from others.

Another interesting unhealthy pairing of emotional energy comes with *Interrogator* and *Aloof* type personas. The *Interrogator* finds self-worth from questioning others in a way that raises self-doubt and creates stories that others are doing things wrong. This slightly less aggressive way of bullying is common in the classroom with "put downs" or questioning intended to elevate their own status. The *Aloof* attempts to gain control in the exact opposite way by showing little interest or caring in response to the interaction. A "who cares" strategy and quantification of the questioning as useless annoying nonsense will incense the *Interrogator* and drive her to try even harder.

FIGURE 10.1

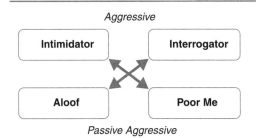

Aggressive

| Intimidator | Interrogator |
| Aloof | Poor Me |

Passive Aggressive

The Celestine Prophecy (Redfield, 1994) identifies control dramas falling on a continuum from the intensely aggressive Intimidator to the very passive *Poor Me*. The commonality of all types is the unhealthy way they attempt to manipulate the energy of others.

When control dramas become chronic, it goes beyond manipulation, winners, and losers. It does not matter who comes out on top because the outcome is always deepening despair for all involved. The emotional high for the winner is only temporary and followed by an emotional crash accompanied by self-loathing, guilt, and depression. The loser of the exchange experiences anxious feelings in response to his loss of control. The natural reaction is to fight back harder by any means possible. For both parties, their unhealthy attachments and insecurities remain in control and increasing emotional manipulation appears to be the only answer. Control dramas escalate, and the cycle of emotional addiction and unhealthy emotional payoffs continues. The competitors are usually unaware of the no-win outcome. The rational part of a person's mind understands that nobody wants to be labeled or remembered as a bully, nag, victim, or uncaring jerk, but her need to garner control by dominating others is powerful and will fight to remain at the expense of her own reputation.

STUDENT–TEACHER CONTROL DRAMAS

In any competition, knowing the other's game plan and objectives is a huge advantage in formulating one's own strategy for the battle ahead. The emotional battles between students and teachers can be complicated, but if teachers can identify the irrational objectives of a control drama, they know exactly where they do not want to go. Sharing relaxed energy and consciously steering students toward connected emotions and thought patterns is the only win-win outcome.

Student Control Drama Game Plans

Intimidator. Students know they will lose this one. They are not in a position to come out a victor in a fight of any sort. The emotional pain of a conflict they will undoubtedly lose and the punishment that follows is what they unconsciously seek. This was Johnny's drama of choice.

Interrogator. A lawyer persona emerges and turns questions back on the teacher to prove they are wrong or unjust. There is a clear intention to elevate their status over the teacher, but it is generally not a winnable strategy either. The emotional debate is what matters.

Aloof. The *Aloof* receives great reward dancing around rules and questioning with an "I don't care" attitude. They achieve victory when teachers no longer have time or energy to maintain the battle. They are the frustrating time stealers in the class.

Poor Me. At first glance their ploys for sympathy may seem harmless and easy to brush off, but the *Poor Me* is an expert at escalating feelings of guilt. If this tactic falls short, a more consciously malicious strategy involves recruiting the sympathy of others in an attempt to demonize the teacher and damage relationships teachers share with other students. Passive can have a mean side.

THINK ABOUT IT

At some point, every teacher is drawn into an emotionally charged conflict. What strategy has thrown you out of balance in the battle for control?

Engaging in a battle with a teacher who holds all the cards is a formidable task, and students may feel that their dominant strategy is not getting the desired results. If unhealthy emotional payoffs are insufficient, students may desperately bounce to other strategies in an attempt to dominate in some other way or escalate the emotional energy. When anger does not garner the desired result, shifting to *Poor Me* energy or the *Aloof* strategy is a predictable response. Recognizing the game strategy in play helps teachers stay grounded and prevent unhealthy emotions from spiraling out of control.

Conflict is always about unhealthy emotions and control. Behavior is just a sideshow that distracts from the underlying drive for unhealthy emotional payoffs. To win in a connected way, a person has to step out of the control drama arena and bring their competition with them. There are no real victors in control dramas so the only alternative is shifting to a connected game of authentic emotions creating win-win feelings of support and safety.

Attempting to solve problems by throwing bad energy at them always distances both players from authentic truth and homeostasis. Sending energy of love, support, and understanding with the intention to make the other feel safe and valued is the only effective response. To do so, one has to let go of the intent to dominate or control. This necessitates an awareness of our own emotional energy we project.

If people are consciously aware of their tendencies when they are knocked out of emotional balance, it becomes possible to effectively deal with control dramas and starve rather than feed unhealthy emotions that drive conflict.

Teachers and the Emotional Blind Spot

Most people are unaware of the predominate energy they send out. Teachers have an authentic intention to share emotional energy that makes their students feel comfortable and safe. They are in the business of support, and it is easy to view themselves from this perspective only. Viewed from a student's standpoint, the starting point may be somewhat different. A teacher is in a position of power, sets the rules, and is unitarily responsible for discipline. Anybody would naturally feel intimidated or manipulated under those parameters. A moderate shift in a teacher's mood is amplified significantly.

On bad days, it is possible for any teacher to lose patience and temporarily slip into their dominant control drama persona. The Intimidator *(angry teacher) persona has shown its ugly face at some point for every teacher. They rarely feel good about this, and emotions of regret or shame usually steer them away from this type of control drama.*

The energy or strategy more commonly projected by teachers is *Interrogation*. It is less aggressive than the *Intimidator* and more palatable for most teachers as an acceptable control strategy. This style embraces rules and arguments that ultimately find fault in the students who break them. It aligns nicely with traditional perceptions of order and control in the classroom.

The least common control dramas employed by teachers are the *Poor Me* or *Aloof* personas because they would be completely ineffectual and simply too painful to endure. A *Poor Me* would invite trouble from *Intimidator* students creating unsafe conditions. An *Aloof* teacher "I don't care" attitude would certainly result in chaos as standards plummet and structure disintegrates. Others in the profession usually perceive these teachers as the weakest in the school. The anxiety of rule-obsessed *Interrogator* teachers observing from across the hall struggle to watch the perpetual chaos.

RULES ARE MADE TO BE BROKEN

If the predominant persona a teacher drifts toward is the *Interrogator*, the *Aloof* student naturally becomes the arch rival. In this scenario, students feel constantly monitored by questions intended to prove classroom rules are just and their behavior is wrong. An *Aloof* response can be an effective means to put teachers back on their heels.

Few things are more frustrating than a one-word, cryptic answer that clearly evades a teacher's objective and intentionally invites more probing questions or clarification of rules. An *Aloof* response is a perfect strategy to gain control from the *Interrogating* teacher and drive him to up his game with more ineffective lecturing and a futile quest to clarify rules. A determined teacher may be able to create a convincing case enforcing a particular rule or appropriate behavior, but a fatal flaw in the strategy emerges.

Rules create helpful guidelines for balanced students, but they play right into the hand of the *Aloof* student. Breaking a rule is a quick way to earn an unhealthy payoff, but it comes with the price of losing control when punishment or scorn follows. Dodging or walking the line of rules is perhaps the most powerful and accessible way for relatively powerless students to invoke and win a control drama with their teacher.

A clearly defined rule and the threat of discipline may make students avoid a behavior, but it does not stop them from intentionally walking to the edge of acceptability. Acting out in another way, not specifically managed by other rules, is just as easy. It would take a very long list of rules to cover every possible behavior scenario. Even if this were possible, the *Aloof* would not care. Skillfully riding the line of appropriate behavior will ascertain her greatest payoff. The best at the game know exactly where the line is, stand on the edge, and taunt their opponent. This knocks teachers off balance, leaving them perpetually guessing when they should justifiably intervene with chronic grey area behaviors. When a teacher does, he should expect a debate.

Teachers trapped guessing whether behaviors fall within the parameters of intended rules will never win because they are playing the wrong game. The questions they need to ask themselves are less ambiguous. Is the behavior or feeling of manipulation chronic, and is it being driven by unhealthy attachments, survival mode responses, or emotional addictions? What kind of emotional payoff is being pursued?

All behavior matters because it offers clues about what is happening in the emotional backdrop of a child's life. Any particular behavior can be determined if it is healthy or not only by resolving what side of the addictive-homeostatic equation it falls on. If students sarcastically say, "Fine then, I'll do it," they may be complying with a desired behavior but it is certainly being driven by a *Poor Me* attachment. Students using language or questioning in a way that puts others down but does not quite cross the line of behavioral expectations are still bullying by interrogation. They know exactly what they are doing, and so does the teacher. There is no grey area or question about emotional intent. Moving forward begins with truth and naming the game being played.

If students pass judgment with borderline acceptable behavior, they are winning the game. There is no such line or grey area when it comes to intent. They want to create drama or they do not. If emotional intent and energy is in question, a teacher's gut feeling can be trusted. The control drama game is easy to sense, and adjusting the perspective can shift the focus from controlling dysfunctional behavior to strategies grounded in healthy emotions, ownership, and choice.

Behavior Is Always a Choice

Making good choices while in survival mode is always a challenge. It is almost a certainty that poor ones will be made. Healthy, life-changing decisions are rarely made when people are anxious or in the heated moments of a control drama. However, when escalated emotions subside, it is one of the best times for emotional healing and facilitation of a choice that pushes students toward a more connected and rewarding authentic life. Teachers just have to be patient and not demand resolution too soon. The perception that a control battle continues or has recommenced can destroy the most honest efforts by teachers. Sometimes, it is a teacher's own unhealthy emotional energy that needs a little time for resolution and de-escalation.

When stress hormones recede and raw emotions have run their course, students are emotionally tired and with a little help they can understand that their choices, drama, and behaviors have led them to a place of uncomfortable emotional pain. In that moment, they are living with the indisputable evidence that proves their coping strategy does not make sense. Chronic emotional pain is not a pleasurable thing. Denying the cause and effect behind their discomfort is a difficult story to rationalize. Like the drug addict hitting rock bottom, they are receptive to the idea of a more connected emotionally balanced life.

An authentic true-self choice coming with the promise of feel-good payoffs sounds quite appealing as a rational alternative, but the false-self lies students live with may run deep, and there is a high probability they will need help uncovering what connection and true-self mean to them. This is the time when teachers armed with a believable story of authentic truth are in an advantageous position. The easy part of painting an authentic true-self story is that the vast majority of connection wants and needs are similar for all students, and we can make certain truthful assumptions in spite of their superficial differences and emotional dysfunction.

Johnny and Ms. G

The Crash Revisited

The Johnny incident, as it had become known, seemed a distant memory. Susan had never experienced an emotional nightmare like it before or since, but she was strangely grateful it happened. The boy seemed so much happier, and she remembered with great love in her heart the moment it all began.

He looked at her with the most desperately tired eyes she had ever seen.

"Please just leave me alone."

His face fell into his hands as he began to cry again.

Being alone was the last thing he wanted. There was no hesitation or thought as she slid her arms around the student she had undeniably hated earlier that day. He was a student in pain. Susan would never see Johnny as a monster again. There had to be an answer.

It took a while for him to calm himself. When the moment felt right, she placed her two fingers under his chin and lifted his head slowly until his teary, red eyes met her own. He was raw and vulnerable. He needed hope. She spoke slowly, crafting her thoughts with great care. Authentic emotions dripped from her every word.

"Johnny, you feel terrible right now but it doesn't have to be this way. You need to hear something I know to be true, so listen carefully.

"You want to belong.

"You want to contribute.

"You want to learn.

"You want to be your best.

"These are things we all need to be happy. We need friends. They make us feel good when we are down, and it feels even better to return the favor. I promise, Johnny, there is a glorious life out there just for you, and it begins with a conscious choice. Be your best and make a difference, happiness will follow.

"It took a horrible stressful moment to discover who you are not. It is time to take control and choose your truth."

The only truth Johnny knew for sure was that he hated his life and wanted something different. Maybe he didn't really believe people would think he was good, but he had nothing to lose. On the worst day of his life, he made a conscious choice to be better.

Connected choices always begin with a story of *truth*. Fortunately, even the most disconnected or dysfunctional have a true-self story. It may be deeply hidden, but it is always there if a person chooses to look for it. For those courageous enough to seek it out, authentic behaviors, beliefs, and payoffs will follow (see Figure 10.2). Choose to feed the Good Wolf!

Believing common authentic truths belong to even the most disruptive students always has to be the starting point. If we cannot get past our own beliefs that a student is worthless, mean, or lazy, there really isn't any point in moving forward.

FIGURE 10.2

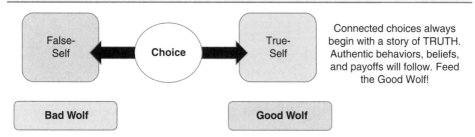

A more optimistic outlook gives teachers hope. This is something students can sense and hold on to as their own.

The most powerful true-self stories a teacher can nurture are more personalized and give a sense that somebody actually cares. This is when authentic student-teacher relationships are truly valuable. When teachers can pull from their pockets a specific and vivid memory of a wonderful moment in the life of a child, the first chapter of a believable connected story is revealed. The evidence is real. "Remember the time you helped Inubu. That must have been amazing and felt really good."

For truly disconnected kids, that healthy behavior moment or redeeming quality may be elusive, but authentic truth always remains. History may not be there, but authentic hopes and dreams always exist somewhere. Gentle, supportive questioning can start the new story. True-self exercises done at the start of the year can give amazing insight into hopes, talents, and passions that may otherwise go unnoticed. Give them a close look. When needed most, the information may prove invaluable.

Control dramas can push students and teachers alike toward emotional imbalance. A teacher's authentic intentions and plans can quickly be lost when emotions escalate. A structured game plan enables teachers to stay the course and help students discover and embrace an authentic true-self choice (see table below).

NURTURING AN AUTHENTIC CHOICE

1. De-escalate control dramas with awareness and relaxed healthy energy.
2. Nurture a story of authentic truth as a more attractive alternative.
3. Take advantage of unhealthy feelings. Expose the cause and effect of false-self beliefs and behaviors. It doesn't feel good. That is undeniable truth.
4. Identify how the behavior defines who they are not (false-self).
5. Free of coercion, control, or threat, facilitate an authentic choice.
6. Monitor and celebrate authentic choices, intentions, and behaviors.

There are a few caveats to this process. The first is that the safety of the tribe trumps all. In the case of severe intimidation or bullying, it is important to name the game and take an immediate stance on unacceptable behavior and distance the drama or danger from others. Class members need to know their safety is an unconditional expectation. The process of reconnection and emotional alignment can continue in a separate, safer environment when emotions recede.

Another caveat is that an authentic choice is an all-or-none proposition of intent to act in connected ways and contribute to the betterment of all. A noncommittal effort falls completely in the realm of the addictive drive. Half-hearted attempts always come with unhealthy payoffs, and a teacher's gut feelings and intuition will always recognize this. On the flip side, authenticity is even easier to read when good choices are made. Teachers need to trust their instincts and be firm with their call. Accepting any degree of control drama is confusing.

A student struggling to make the commitment may need more help refining authentic thinking patterns or a more powerful story of truth. This does not change the stance that connections with the tribe are a privilege and the price is authentic intent. There is always room for slip-ups or mistakes, but inauthentic games that steal healthy energy or make a mockery of connection intentions are unacceptable.

CONSEQUENCE

If, after efforts to nurture awareness and healthy thinking patterns, students hang on to destructive false-self beliefs, they have to live with the choices they have made. Have students work on their own or find a spot to rethink their emotional intent. The irrationality of their decision usually becomes apparent. One more chance without serious intent is enabling at its worst.

It is important to make it clear that isolation is not a punishment. It is a product of their choice and an opportunity to reflect on it. This distinction gives them ownership of their actions. This limits the control dramas that will inevitably emerge as they attempt to navigate the relationship between their feelings and behaviors.

Students should be free to return to class activities when they conclude and decide authentic connection is a better choice. Again, a teacher's intuition will always recognize the making of an authentic choice and intention. Be firm with games, and take the power of choice away if they do not make an authentic one. This is still a choice that they own. If disconnection is so severe that she cannot make an authentic choice, alternative environments with a different energy may become the only option until the student rebalances. Rules, control, and punishments-type strategies fall short of lasting authentic attachment objectives. Perceived successes will undoubtedly be fleeting and may even inhibit the type of attachments that ultimately change behaviors in a lasting way.

Rules and punishment are temporary. Connection is forever.

Everyday Behavior Management

The most effective and lasting behavior management strategy is nurturing healthy attachments and supportive environments. Out-of-line behavior will creep into even the most connected classrooms. Any student can temporarily fall out of balance and need a gentle nudge or reminder.

Testing limits of acceptable behavior is part of learning and growing, and to some degree should be encouraged. Making mistakes is inevitable. Sometimes students have to experience right and wrong, process their feelings, and resolve the scenario with thoughtful reflection and action. Many of life's great lessons come from natural but emotionally painful responses to social experiences and behaviors that stretch boundaries and go wrong. Students need room to make mistakes, process uncomfortable emotions, and manage their problems.

> *Uncomfortable feelings are nature's way of trying to teach students a lesson.*
> Mother Nature

Teachers are behavior management experts. They have to be. They come armed with a toolbox full of strategies, making their classroom feel safe and run smoothly. Teachers skillfully use these tools to help students turn negative emotions and behaviors into meaningful learning opportunities. However, when those lessons are not learned, and behaviors continue to disrupt learning, a closer look at what drives the behavior may be necessary.

Behavior Management and Connection Hierarchy

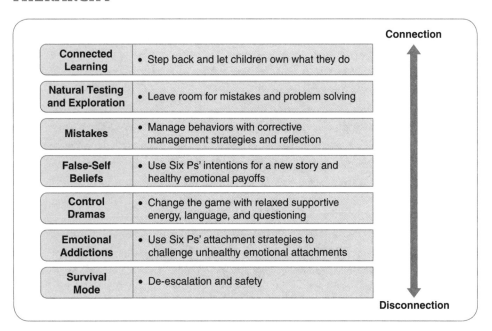

Using a hammer when a screwdriver makes more sense would certainly make a carpenter's task at hand a challenge. Choosing the proper tool would be a better plan. The same is true when managing the behaviors, beliefs, and emotions of students. Effective strategies begin with understanding behavior for what it really is and choosing an appropriate course of action. A threat of punishment or isolation when a simple nudge to correct a thoughtless mistake would do is overkill and may trigger unnecessary painful emotions. A hands-off approach to emotional addictions that drive chronically dangerous behaviors would be even more hazardous. Where behavior sits on the connection-disconnection spectrum dictates the appropriate course of action. Understanding the subtleties of human behavior elevates the potential to transform lives. Knowing what to do and when to do it empowers teachers with their own sense of control and allows them to step back from unhealthy behaviors and support students from a neutral, practical perspective.

Alice

"The Pleaser," An Unusual Addiction

After cleaning the whiteboard, Alice placed the eraser back neatly on the ledge. As she made her way back to her desk, a quiet whisper caught her attention.

"You're such a suck up."

It may have been soft enough to evade the ear of Ms. G, but for Alice it echoed loudly as she lowered her head and took a seat. The little jab stung deeply. Only the truth had been spoken. This frustrated her because she tried hard to do things to make others like her. She was very smart but could not seem to figure out what others expected of her.

The exception to that rule was with her parents. There was significant pressure to do well at school and eventually attend a prestigious university. They had made many personal sacrifices and worked very hard to provide a good life for their daughter. The road to success was paved with a strong, focused work ethic and personal sacrifice. It was a lesson that often came up when she eased off on homework. Letting her parents down was not an option.

She appreciated her parents' efforts, but she wished they had more time to spend together. They worked long hours, and most of her time consisted of studying alone in her room. The little conversation typically shared revolved around schoolwork. Her parents rarely got excited about anything other than her numerous academic awards, so that is where she put her time and energy. She knew her parents loved her, but sometimes it felt conditional on her grades. What if she failed? The thought made her heart sink.

The sweet voice of Ms. Grabowski startled her out of the painful reflection of her life.

"Thank you for cleaning the board. I really appreciate it."

Despite her frustration Alice forced out a smile and returned a "You're welcome."

She straightened up her back to strengthen the illusion that all was well, but the truth remained. Despite her efforts, contentment and happiness seemed more elusive than ever. The connections, laughter, and excitement in the classroom were real for others. It wasn't fair. She was a good person and deserved better.

In the back of the class, Johnny and the new boy noisily bounced about as they joyfully worked on their recycling project. She knew her presentation would receive a higher mark, but that did little to stem the jealousy fueled by the pair's unbridled friendship. It only got worse when Ms. G made her way across the class to settle them down. There was something so special about the bond between Ms. G and Johnny. She had a way of turning up the love when Johnny needed it, and his troubles just seemed to melt away.

She didn't like to feel resentment toward a wonderful teacher like Ms. Grabowski, but the same caring feelings just never seemed to greet her in such a natural way. She was a good kid, and it did not make sense to her.

The boy beside Johnny confused her even more. He existed in a world she just could not comprehend. He struggled with studies but didn't appear to have a care in the world. Joy and passion poured out from deep within and drew others toward him like a magnet. What did he have that made others like him so much? She would gladly trade all her awards just to experience his life for a moment. Why was it all so easy for him? Maybe she was just a person who couldn't be happy. Alice took a deep breath and returned to her work.

Later that evening Alice continued to dutifully work on her project in the quiet of her room, but her thoughts kept drifting back to the passion and happiness Johnny and Inubu shared earlier in the day. There was the option to work with a partner, but like usual, she would have ended up doing all the work anyway. She was the top student in the class, and she worried their input might lower her own grade.

She reluctantly convinced herself that working with somebody else would end up feeling awkward anyway. The stories she told herself didn't really change the fact that deep down she wanted to experience adventure and excitement with passionate friends, but something inside held her back from letting go and embracing life in the way others did.

She wasn't sure when it happened, but she soon found herself singing softly to a lovely song that was playing on her laptop. It felt good, and a small authentic smile crept across her face. Alice rose from her bed to look in the mirror to prove it was real. The smile was different from the one she used to hide her sadness from others.

Her voice was surprisingly pleasant, and she continued to softly sing and dance for some time. When she heard the front door open and close, she knew her parents were home. She quickly turned off the music and got back to work on her project. She felt bitter about it all. She deserved to be happy and couldn't understand why nobody seemed to care.

Alice was a songbird. A songbird who would never find her true voice.

Ms. Grabowski

Alice appeared to be doing just fine, but a little closer look might have spotted the smile that wasn't quite right. It would devastate Susan to discover that she had overlooked a student in need. A student unable to find true passion and experience authentic connections could never be happy. Alice was good at hiding her pain, and Ms. G would never know it.

CHAPTER 11

A Bold Proclamation for Change

A connected life is joyful and optimistic. It doesn't really matter what is going on in the disconnected world around us. Life is complicated only if we choose to make it so. Obsessing about things beyond our control or pursuing inauthentic desires that do not really matter at all takes a great deal of work. Hard work that inevitably leads to distress and emotional pain.

Fortunately, we always own the step in front of us. Nothing can take that away unless we allow it to do so. Live in the moment, love those around us, share healthy energy, and stay connected with the things that matter most. Happiness is that easy. So is the choice to embrace it. Only we control our destiny.

The same is true of our classrooms. Curriculum, expectations, test scores, and unnecessary details of the day can overwhelm us. We love our kids, we know they deserve better, and that is difficult to accept. We feel bad, because we make the wrong choice too often. The good news is that it does not have to be that way.

Teachers drawn to the profession come with an authentic desire to make a difference. Most of this book is simply about using a new lens to view what we already do really well from a more connected perspective. Despite this truth, forging a new path always comes with a certain amount of anxiety and doubt. Every day we ask our children to be brave, dive in, and embrace challenge. They watch and learn from us. Connection in the classroom begins with the choices we make for ourselves. Learning connection demands that it is lived. Be brave, and make your own bold proclamation for a connected life and educational change.

Classrooms offer a unique opportunity to influence the lives of children like no other. The educational community in its entirety knows there is a problem, and there is an overwhelming consensus that doing things the way we always have isn't working. The winds of change are upon us, and the door is opening, but waiting for guidance or permission from the experts above or new progressive curriculums remains a non-choice. Connection in the classroom never comes from somewhere else. It comes from the teacher who knows exactly what his students need. This is why many broad-based connection initiatives show modest results. Connection is a personal thing that starts with a truthful commitment of a single teacher.

Imagine playing a part in liberating just one emotionally distressed child from the debilitating effects of lifelong attachments to emotional pain. That would be a big deal and certainly worth the effort, but fixing sad or dysfunctional is not the point of this book. It is about enabling happiness for all our students and teaching them to share it with others. If there is a defining purpose for why we teach, this is it.

Hundreds or even thousands of students will sit in desks in front of yours. Imagine letting go of all the superfluous matters that fall within our perceived duties and focusing on the only lesson that really counts: how to live a happy, fulfilling, and purposeful life. Imagine harder, that years from now when your students become parents themselves, that they share those same lessons at home with their children. Imagine harder still that your passionate quest is passed on to another teacher and then another, who then deliver the message to the thousands of children in front of them. This is the power of connection. This is how the world changes for the better.

Standing at the fork in the road always comes with a question. You can gaze into the distance, but you can't see what lies at the end. It is impossible to discern but stories of an unknown future matter little. It is only the first connected step that matters. Connection and healthy emotions will always tell you where to go, and they will always take you to a place of happiness.

FINAL WORDS: A TEACHER'S GREATEST GIFT

It is easy to lose track of the important things in life when superfluous demands seem to pile up and consume us. Life is far easier than we make it. It is in our nature to love and be loved, to give and graciously receive. In this lies the motivation that pushes us to be our best. We are teachers, and we know what makes us happy. We teach and give, because that is what makes us feel good.

Our students need us more than ever in this confusing, disconnected world. There is no excuse when a child leaves school not knowing what makes them feel happy and fulfilled. Teaching children to discover and pursue what makes them feel good and emotionally balanced is the only lesson that really matters. It is the greatest gift we can give. It is a gift that will live on far after we are retired and gone.

Epilogue
Prayers in a Food Truck

Years after the war, the refugee camp, and his graduation from school, Inubu busily shuffled around the back of his food truck chopping vegetables and mixing spices for the day ahead. He spent long hours here and worked very hard to enjoy a moderately successful business. Customers could count on a laugh and always left with a piece of his incredibly contagious smile. For many of his loyal regulars consumption of the simple food was an afterthought. Inubu sensed this but remained proud of his culinary efforts.

The joyful songs of birds and the early morning sunlight filtered through the tiny windows of the truck and brought warmth to his spirit. It was at this moment each day he took the time to say a few prayers.

The first prayer was a gesture of thanks for his loved ones long past and the gifts they left behind. His beloved uncle taught him that a warrior does not fight, he protects. The emotional last words of his father rarely drifted far from his thoughts. They shaped much of his life that followed. His path was clear. Through giving he could make a difference, and the belief revealed a greatness in himself he never imagined possible. These simple lessons were always with him and guided him through difficult times no boy should endure, but he was thankful those same teachings were responsible for all the love and happiness shared in his wonderful life.

His thoughts drifted to where it all began. The fragrant smoke of the village campfire danced among the sounds of unrestrained laughter as young and old villagers shared in joyful songs and rich, entertaining stories of adventure. This is where he learned to love and be loved. He missed them all deeply, but their love and memories filled the hole in his heart in the best way imaginable.

His second prayer was one of gratefulness for the life he had lived. Perhaps his role in the world had been modest, but he knew what made him happy and did his best to share his love. Maybe he had fallen short of his grand childhood dreams, but he couldn't deny that his choices and humble contributions to the lives of his loved ones felt big.

His memories of school were fond despite the difficult standards. Graduation with his newfound friends was a special moment. He wasn't a doctor, lawyer, or politician capable of changing the world. He wasn't famous, rich, or powerful. Inubu only worked in a food truck, but the lessons learned had served him well. They provided the will, guidance, and inspiration to persevere, stay true, and in his own way make the world a little better. He was still just a boy when he had put his own life at risk without thought. Protecting and caring for his family was all that had ever mattered, and now his hard work in a simple food truck provided a comfortable life for them all. It wasn't much, but he knew his father would be proud.

Satisfaction filled his heart when he thought of his now grown brother. The little one was much younger when he entered school and, unlike Inubu, had flourished academically. He later went on to university and graduated at the top of his class. The same child he had carried so far, the one who almost died on the doorstep of the refugee camp, was now working as a doctor in Africa helping others who struggled with a common misfortune. In this story, Inubu had indeed played an immeasurable role. He was not the boy's father, but he also always did his best to play the part.

A third and final prayer spoke of the life he now lived and hope for the future. He was happy, and his joy for giving was always accompanied by great love from others. His best friend Johnny had unexpectedly gifted him the money for the truck that supported his family. Inubu tried to pay him back when business took off, but Johnny just laughed and then whispered in his most sincere voice.

"Thanks, but payment was already made a long time ago."

Johnny was a kind and gentle man and a popular high school teacher. Inubu hoped the students knew how fortunate they were. He could not imagine a better teacher, mentor, or friend.

The journey had been worthwhile, and he hoped for a long life to love and laugh with old and new friends, but he had been through enough to know that nothing in life is a certainty. All he knew for sure was that the connections and memories he had shared in the life he had lived would endure. Thoughts of love turned to his beautiful wife and expectations of their soon to be born first child. For now, time was on his side and every day was worth his best.

It was time to open for business. He pushed up the metal slider and welcomed the beautiful day with his equally beautiful smile. Life was good and the future was bright.

Connection Intentions and the Six Ps

"I will make my life and the lives of those around me better by choosing to embrace and share healthy emotions, beliefs, and behaviors at the start of each day."

PEOPLE

SHARE HEALTHY ENERGY

- **Smiles, laughter, and fun are contagious:** *Be fun. Model, teach, and practice the skills of fun.*

- **Be a great cheerleader:** *Celebrate when others take risk, fail, or achieve best efforts. Model, teach, and practice the skills of cheerleading.*

- **Practice communication skills:** *Get specific. Model and integrate specific healthy communication skills in everyday lessons. Begin with checklists to guide behaviors.*

- **Change the intention from doing to feeling:** *Saying good words or doing good things has minimal impact without emotion. Practice* *wrapping words in real feelings. Reflect on how social exchanges feel when the emotional volume is turned up.*

BE SOCIAL

- **Nurture new connections:** *Partner up with someone new.*

- **Practice social skills in the community:** *Make a stranger feel good by sharing a healthy greeting. While on a neighborhood nature walk for science class, take a moment to tell a dog owner their beloved pet is cute (even if it is not, it will make the owner feel happy!). If the connection intent is pure, it is OK to stretch things a little.*

- **Embrace school culture:** *Discuss opportunities to embrace school culture outside the classroom (clubs, teams, volunteering). Set an intention to try one out. Report back on your progress.*

DIVE IN AND TAKE SOCIAL RISK

- **Process social mistakes in healthy ways:** *Social mistakes filtered through healthy thinking are funny and are a symbol of social humility, bravery, and resilience. People like funny and brave. Embrace it. Try a swing dance lesson. It offers plenty of social challenge and opportunities to process mistakes.*

COMMUNAL SUCCESS

- **Think team, communal goals. Great leaders elevate the game of the team:** *Value the assist. It's still a goal if someone else scores it.*

- **Strive for shared understanding:** *Try a cooperative test.*

- **Value the opinions and efforts of others:** *Think-Pair-Share.*

COMMUNAL SAFETY SUPPORT

- **Think communal safety:** *Make a formal intent or pledge for collective safety.*

- **Be an active protector:** *Try a lesson that puts the onus for physical or emotional safety in the hands of students.*

- **We are here to help others:** *Perhaps more important, others are here to help you. Embrace help, protection, and support as a strength, not a weakness. It is an undervalued aspect of community building and communal success.*

VALUE THE OPINIONS, PERSPECTIVES, AND UNIQUE QUALITIES OF OTHERS

- **Value the opinions of others:** *Practice sharing opinions and reaching consensus. Workable compromise and communal intent bring harmony to the tribe and provide innovative solutions for challenges.*

- **Value the perspectives of others:** *Practice solving conflicts or problems from the perspective of others. Tell the "Three Little Pigs" story from the perspective of the wolf. He is not evil; he starves if he doesn't eat. How does the lesson relate to how classmates experience learning? How does it relate to world conflict? Understanding increases the capacity to support and solve problems.*

- **Value cultural identities:** *Cultural identity is an important part of truth. Value differences and share them. Tell stories, read books, eat new food, sing anthems, or engage in learning projects that elevate the value of different cultures. Different is exciting and interesting. Content and ideas are limitless. Celebrate differences.*

- **Value the differences in others:** *Interview a friend. Find out what makes her unique and special. Be an interested listener.*

- **Learn in culturally responsive ways:** *Teach a content lesson in a manner that reflects the learning styles of different cultures. This may include story telling, songs, drumming, dance, art, or learning through doing. This intention is not an informative lesson about different cultures. It focuses on acknowledging, respecting and celebrating how other cultures learn. Culturally responsive learning brings content to life.*

PURPOSE

CONTRIBUTE TO THE GREATER GOOD

- **Always seek to make your classroom better:** *When no other intention is set, this mantra will always send a student in a good direction.*

- **Seek out classmates in need:** *Be intuitive, read the energy of others, especially those you do not know well.*

- **Make meaningful contributions to family, community, or environment:** *Design a project that positively impacts the world beyond the classroom.*

- **Help and graciously accept help:** *Healthy payoffs flow in both directions. Assess the emotional energy you shared.*

- **Hard work:** *Effort and being your best increases the potential to contribute, acknowledge, and assess effort.*

VALUE YOURSELF

- **You are great only if you share it. Trust that you have something to contribute:** *Be brave and share what you know or can do.*

- **Contribution is an authentic measure of worth. Measure it!** *Today I made a difference in this way.*

- **Critical and creative thought:** *Often considered the benchmark for meaningful learning. New ideas or opinions are an asset for the greater good and offer significant payoffs for feelings of self-worth. Reflect on the feelings a critical or creative thought provides rather than the A grade or product generated.*

VALUE OTHERS

- **Valuing others:** *Involve others in a task that matters to you.*

- **Practice supportive language:** *Practice supportive language. Compliments feel good. A kind and thoughtful critique feels great for both parties. Practice the compliment sandwich.*

- **Embrace the uniqueness of others:** *Value the synergy of employing partners with different attributes, skill sets, or talents. This is not about* *stacking the team. A unique passion or talent can unexpectedly come from anyone and make an experience better. A student with special needs may possess beautiful energy and offer the group an unsuspected source of motivation to be better.*

- **Team thinking:** *Building a team is more valuable than any specific task or goal. Use a goal or challenge to strengthen the spirit of team and the skills sets and/or thinking patterns of all team members. It is a worthy investment for future endeavors.*

COACHING

- **Be the best coach you can be:** *Create checklists and procedures that help students be good coaches.*

    - **Model good practice habits:** *Stick to the coaching plan.*

    - **Set high standards:** *Always shoot for your partners' true-self best efforts. Low standards are easy and comfortable but offer only an illusion of kindness. Be firm with standards that reflect a peer's potential.*

    - **Be knowledgeable:** *Make an effort to know the key teaching points well.*

    - **Share healthy energy:** *If the task is challenging, your partner may need healthy energy to help them through it. Energy flows downhill, so be prepared to share healthy emotional energy with your partner, especially when it is difficult. Patience and kindness is a wonderful gift.*

    - **Be intuitive:** *Monitor, analyze, and adapt to the emotional energy that comes back to you. Assess yourself by the emotional feedback you receive.*

    - **Leave the EGO at home!** *Strive to help others, not to be better than them.*

- **You do not have to be great at something to be a great coach:** *Teach something you do not know well. Studying the simple key points and sharing healthy energy can go far.*

Play

COOPERATION, CREATIVITY, RESPONSIBILITY, AND RESILIENCY

- **Free play is fun and inspiring:** *Loosen parameters of learning structures to allow room for children to freely develop and share new creative ideas.*

- **Free play is emotionally balancing:** *Structure time for free play for the sake of sharing healthy emotional energy.*

- **Encourage playful physicality:** *Embrace nature's path to resilience and toughness.*

- **Play reduces competition:** *Turn competitive tasks into cooperative playful experiences. It reduces anxiety and fosters social skills.*

- **Play reduces fear:** *Playful energy is the enemy of fear. Sing like nobody is watching, and laugh at mistakes.*

- **Active learning:** *Get moving. The brain responds better to doing than listening alone.*

- **Playful exercise:** *Embrace the endorphins that come with exercise.*

- **Singing changes the brain:** *Learn through song. Song enhances listening skills and language acquisition in young children. All ages benefit from improved memorization of material.*

- **Play encourages problem solving and creative thinking:** *Children are responsible for their own discoveries during free play. Present a task or problem, stand clear, and give time for the process.*

- **Encourage responsibility and sense of fairness through play:** *Allow children to create their own rules for games and learning. Trust and give children the opportunity to develop their natural sense of fairness and responsibility.*

- **Encourage moderately dangerous physical play and risk:** *Physicality is the most natural form of animal play. Run, climb, wrestle and get dirty to learn physical skills and nurture toughness and resiliency.*

Passions, Talents, and Interests

EMBRACE YOUR PASSIONS, INTERESTS, AND TALENTS, AND EXPERIENCE BIG FEELINGS

- **Embrace a passion or interest purely for the sake of pleasure:** *Passions trigger big healthy emotional payoffs (endorphins) that help us rebalance.*

- **Passions and interests always come with healthy payoffs:** *Wrap learning in your favorite passion or pastime to elevate motivation and interest.*

- **Express learning or the process of learning through your favorite interest, passion, or pastime:** *Art, singing, technology, drama, hobbies, or unique talents can add interest and healthy emotions to curricular objectives that may otherwise be less than inspiring.*

- **Genius hour:** *Set aside an hour a week to explore passions and interests. Try a yearlong project with as few strings attached as possible.*

BEING DIFFERENT IS VALUABLE TO THE GREATER GROUP

- **Different is a good thing!** *Share a unique talent passion or interest that nobody else can. This makes you invaluable for expanding the outlook and learning of the group. It is also a healthy way to nurture feelings of self-worth.*

PRACTICE THE SKILLS OF PASSION AND ENTHUSIASM

- **Share a passionate story:** *Read or tell a story with dripping passion.*

- **Debate a controversial topic:** *It's not about winning or losing, but choose enthusiasm and authentic argument over facts for the win!*

- **Be a great cheerleader:** *Some people struggle to celebrate their own achievements. Practice the skills of being a great cheerleader for someone else. It is a great way to train the brain to let it out when they are ready to celebrate their amazing self.*

PRESENT THINKING

EMBRACE TRUTH

- **The Six Ps and personal inventories:** *Use the Six Ps and personal inventory exercises to reveal a sense of authentic self. Use true-self targets to create a personalized roadmap leading toward health, wellness, and happiness.*

- **Embrace your truth:** *The anxiety of uncomfortable challenge will always attempt to create false stories and drag students into a failure or "poor me" mindset. Prepare children for challenging moments by arming them with truthful mantra's to keep them balanced. I am safe, supported, valued, capable, and brave.*

- **Good Wolf/Bad Wolf:** *The story told by the old Cherokee chief is an excellent metaphor students of any age can use to understand true-self–false-self choices and emotional payoffs. Choosing to feed the Good Wolf is always a great intention for any lesson.*

- **Measure connectedness:** *Are students' behaviors, beliefs, and feelings aligned with how they live their life. Set an intention to measure the connection and/or disconnection in their lives. Chronic disconnections are a sign of unhealthy beliefs, attachments, and potential addictions.*

- **Measure feelings against the learning experience:** *Reflect on feelings students' experience during and after lessons. Feel-good emotions are an indicator for connectedness. Unhealthy feelings or thoughts that linger are a sign that adjustments to activities, environments, thought patterns, or lessons are necessary.*

LIVE IN THE PRESENT MOMENT

- **Anxiety is a time traveler:** *It can tell any painful story it wants in the past or future. Arm students with mindfulness strategies that help them stay grounded in present moment safety. Monitor emotions and thought patterns during lessons to "check in" to the truth of the present moment.*

- **Mindfulness:** *Listen to your body and recognize the signals of unnecessary stress. Employ strategies to manage emotional states.*

- **Choose to be accountable and responsible for choices, behaviors, and feelings:** *Give room for students to own what they do. An intention for accountability and ownership of behaviors, feelings, and the emotional energy they share reminds students that they control their own destiny and the story they share with the world.*

- **Forgiveness:** *Forgive yourself. Forgive others. Letting go of past events that caused anger, guilt, or jealousy is a great way to rebalance. Read a story of forgiveness or take a real step and make it happen in your own life. Reflect on the emotional change.*

FIND YOUR ZONE-ACTIVATION LEVELS

- **Pump it up:** *Stress can help us run faster, think clearer, and get things done quickly. Embrace stress as a good thing to be a better athlete, share a powerful enthusiastic presentation, or meet the deadline for a task. Just don't get too high!*

- **Dial it back:** *Practice relaxation techniques or mindfulness strategies to mitigate unnecessary stress that may impede concentration, performance, or creativity. Just don't get too low!*

- **Find your trigger word:** *Use a personalized trigger word to regain focus. Relax … Jell-O Jell-O Jell-O!*

THINKING PATTERNS OF THE CHAMPIONS: BE POSITIVE

- **Visualization:** *Picture a positive outcome.*

- **Positive self-talk:** *Growth mindset and positive words influence outcome.*

- **Control the controllables:** *Before or during a learning challenge think about the things that may be causing you stress. Split them into matters you can and cannot control at that moment. Focus on and embrace the ones you can. You will be feeding the Good Wolf if you are successful. At the end of the task, assess how you think you did.*

Personal Growth

GROWTH MINDSET

- **Nurture mindsets of belief, big dreams, and growth:** *Hard work and growth mindsets will always push us to a better place.*

- **Set goals and dream big. Set authentic realistic goals:** *Link goals to true-self exercises and embrace a plan. SMART (specific, measurable, achievable, realistic, timely). It is reassuring and comforting to have a plan that creates a story of success.*

VALUE "UNCOMFORTABLE": IT IS AN OPPORTUNITY TO GROW AND BUILD RESILIENCY

- **Emotional discomfort—Plan a learning experience that triggers anxious feelings:** *Wrap the activity in healthy thinking patterns, support, and authentic connections to help students rebalance and celebrate their effort and growth. Classroom presentations, new social scenarios, or learning challenges with the potential for perceived failure will fit the bill.*

- **Physical discomfort. Engage in a physical task that pushes known limits and feels physically uncomfortable or painful (not dangerously so, of course):** *Emotional pain and unhealthy thoughts often accompany physical challenges. An advantage of an uncomfortable physical task is that physical pain goes away when it is over. It is no longer necessary in the same way that the emotional discomfort is also unnecessary. Physical challenge is a great opportunity to practice letting go of the emotional "poor me" pain and unhealthy thoughts of failure. This is a core strategy of many outdoor experiential programs.*

- **Challenge anxious stories and weaknesses:** *Avoiding anxious stories and false beliefs is limiting opportunities for growth and healing. Identify weak spots with belief inventories and go after them. Nothing is more rewarding and liberating than overcoming a fear.*

- **Choose difficult:** *Offer a selection of activities or learning challenges, and encourage students to choose the one they find most challenging. Choosing difficult is much more appealing than having it thrust upon you. Ownership and control are powerful motivators.*

- **Delayed gratification:** *Sometimes practice is boring, but it is always valuable. Keep your eyes on the prize, and find present moment satisfaction in efforts that will pay off in the future. Today I got a little closer to my dream.*

BE BRAVE

- **Dive in and just do it!** *The first step is the one that matters most. Even if failure follows, value it. Bravery is a big deal for real learning. Think bungee jumping. Even if you hated it, the fact that you were brave enough to take the step cannot be taken away from you. Answer the question, even if you are not sure you have it right. Take the shot, or say hello to someone new. What is the worst that can happen? … To experience the regret of not trying.*

- **Be safe:** *Being safe and feeling safe can be two different things. Safety procedures and connections that help student feel safe can be a stand-alone lesson for challenges ahead. All members must share an intention that nurtures a believable story of safety classmates can trust. Nurturing safe stories helps others be brave.*

- **Celebrate mistakes:** *Value mistakes as evidence for bravery. Often it is a fear of judgment by others that makes bravery difficult. Flip the belief by making a daily intention that celebrates mistakes of classmates as a good thing.*

PERSONAL BESTS FEEL AMAZING

- **Try really, really hard:** *Best efforts are never easy but always worth celebrating. Testing is a valuable way to set benchmarks for task improvement or emotional growth. No fluffy compliments please; today may be the day I surprise myself with real effort and accomplishment. Grit matters. It is not the score but the effort that counts.*

RESILIENCY

- **Practice resiliency:** *Train the brain for resiliency in the same way that athletes train their muscles. Discomfort and recovery—over and over again. It is a cliché but true. No pain, no gain.*

Sample Intention Unit Plans/Subject Intentions

ROMEO & JULIET

Connection Intention: Use a classic piece of literature to nurture communication skills and influence others through language. Be brave and passionately share your ideas.

SUPPORTING CONNECTION INTENTIONS

- **Value yourself:** Share ideas, practice communication skills. It feels good to contribute ideas!

- **Be brave, take risk:** Dive in and share your thoughts. Trust that your peers will support you. There is no right or wrong with opinion.

- **Be prepared and deliberate:** Organize ideas into succinct thoughts.

- **Be emotionally accessible and vulnerable**: This is a story of passion. Passion always draws the attention of others. Embrace it!

SOURCE: Madison Watt, 2018 (personal communication)

Volleyball (Pinetree PE Department)

Connection Intention: Be FEARLESS and BOLD: This is a team sport where all members must be involved and committed to improvement of the team.

- Be prepared to move, react quickly, and be involved.

- **Stamp out fear.** Anxiety forces students into avoidance mode. Challenge it! Do not look to others to make the play. Know your role and commit.

- Take the shot and make **big mistakes full on,** that is how you learn. Value that!

- Practice **positive visualization** and positive self-talk.

- **Support teammates** who are willing to **take the risk** to make improvements.

- **Value all members** on your team. Helping them get better makes your team better and the game better.

- **Ask** yourself, **Did I make my team better today** so they are better tomorrow?

Swing Dance

Connection Intention: *Take the fear out of socialization.* Be Brave and Laugh. This is the safe time to be the person you really want to be. Take charge or graciously follow. It's up to you. Just dive in!

- **Make someone feel special.**

  Understand that the positive energy you share can help others be socially brave. It's a wonderful gift!

- Make connections: **Ask for and use names, ask questions, remember the answers!**

- Switch partners: **Maximize your leadership opportunities.**

Your social skills are what make you successful in all areas of life.

- Instead of seeking out your friends, **make someone new feel great!**

- **Be fearless! Mistakes are just funny! Everyone likes funny!**

Source: Rachel Armstrong, 2018 (personal communication)

Connection Intentions for Middle School Math: "Feed the Good Wolf"

1. Make connections: **Ask for help,** give help kindly, and accept help graciously.

2. Seek **support**: When you're stuck, don't give up, and don't stay stuck. Ask a neighbor or the teacher.

3. **Contribute**: Notice and value answers you shared with the group or class.

4. Role **model**: Were you a good example to others. How? For example, staying on task, having your Jump Math Book, white board marker, red pen, homework done, and encouraging others?

5. **Share your expertise**: Let your enthusiasm and knowledge for today's topic enlighten the class.

6. **Grow** your **enthusiasm**: Fake it till you make it. Even though this may not be your favorite activity, bring positive energy, "Let's do this!"

7. Positive **self-talk**: When a negative thought comes into your mind (e.g., I'm going to bomb this test), turn away and look on the bright side. Put this in perspective.

8. **Keep calm and carry on**: When a problem seems difficult, use strategies that allow you to keep going rather than giving up (e.g., sketch the problem, record the numbers you do know, in a formula if possible, check the first step with a friend, etc.).

9. **Challenge yourself to reach a "step"**: Decide at the start of class what a reasonable goal will be by the end of class; did you make it? If yes, celebrate. If no, how will you do it differently next time?

10. **Bravely project your voice**: Could every person in the room hear you when you contributed to a discussion and/or asked a question?

SOURCE: Naomi McDonnell, 2018 (personal communication)

The Kinderbuddy Lesson Plan

Lesson Title: <u>Passionately share your Kinderbuddy story</u>   **Date** _____

- **Connection Intention(s) (Six Ps):** Value your work, and **Passionately** share your story. Use the **Connection skills** practiced to create a joyful experience for your younger peer.

- **Prescribed Learning Outcome(s)**: Create an original children's storybook that demonstrates creative writing and artwork.

HEALTHY ATTACHMENT STRATEGY (AT LEAST ONE SHOULD BE USED EVERY LESSON)

1. Everyday healthy connections: connection skills, people, purpose, play, passion

2. Healthy thinking patterns: mindfulness and connections with authentic truth (Statement of Safety)

3. Challenge, resiliency, and growth: stressful learning challenge, support, and emotional balance

LESSON	NOTES	TIME
Introduction: **Anticipatory set:** You've worked hard on your projects. They look amazing. Today you get to share your story with a very excited Kinderbuddy. **Statement of Safety:** Today is an important day. Being an older peer is a big deal. Your presence will have a significant impact. Value this, and do your best to make it a memorable experience. If you are feeling nervous, there is no need. You are kind and caring and have practiced the skills of connection. Your buddy will look up to you. They will not judge. All they want is your attention. Share it passionately. Take a deep breath and begin with a smile. In return, the attention of your Kinderbuddy will feel amazing.		
Main Activity and Lesson Structure: Review key connection and presentation points: • Share a warm welcome. Big kids can be scary. Be playful! • The emotional energy you share will be assessed—smiles, voice tone, posture, and so on. • Take your time, and passionately share your story. Don't just read it. • Focus on making a Little Friend. **Checking In:** Read the energy of the classes. If it is high, take a moment to celebrate. If it is low, it is probably because they are nervous. Refocus the intention or give specific tips. Hands up responses to questions: • Are we having fun? • Do we have a new friend? • High fives, and get back to the story. **Stamping Behaviors:** Read the faces of the Kinderbuddies. When you see authentic engagement, share a whisper of praise for the storyteller. If a student is challenging a fear, make a note. Look for moments of excellence, and share it with the class. **Activity closure**		
Connection assessment and reflection (measure and celebrate attachment outcomes): Self-assessment score /100 How do students feel about the emotional energy shared? Did you make a Little Friend? Did you have a WOW moment?		
Closure: Celebrate wonderful connections made. Make a link to the lasting impression students have made on their peers. How has the experience influenced the capacity to share good energy?		

Teacher Reflection: How do you feel about the connections that were made during the lesson? How could you improve on the quality of connections next time? _____

References

Allington, R., & McGill-Franzen, A. (1989). School response to reading failure: Chapter 1 and special education students in grades 2, 4, and 8. *Elementary School Jouranal*, 529–542.

Amabile, T. (1996). *Creativity in context: Update to the social psychology of creativity*. Boulder, CO: Westview Press.

Barker, G. (n.d.). The effects of trauma on attachment. Retrieved from http://www.ccaa.net.au/documents/TheEffectsOfTraumaOnAttachment.pdf

Berridge, K., & Robinson, T. (2016). Liking, wanting, and the incentive-sensitization theory of addiction. *American Psychologist*, *71*(8), 670–679.

Blum, R., & Libby, H. (2004). School connectedness executive summary: Strengthening health and educational outcomes for teenagers. *Journal of School Health*, *74*(7), 231–232.

Bowlby, J. (1965). *Child care and the growth of love*. Harmondsworth, UK: Penguin.

Boyd, L. (2015). After watching this your brain will not be the same. TEDx Talk. Retrieved from https://www.youtube.com/watch?v=LNHBMFCzznE

Centers for Disease Control and Prevention. (2016). Quickstats: Death rates for motor vehical traffic injury, suicide, and homocide among children and adolescents aged 10–14 years—United States, 1999–2014. *Morbidity and Mortality Weekly Reort*, *65*(43), 1203.

Collishaw, S., Maughan, B., Natarajan, L., & Pickles, A. (2010). Trends in adolescent emotional problems in England: a comparison of two national cohorts twenty years apart. *Journal of Child Psychology and Psychiatry*, *51*(8), 885–894.

Dweck, C. (2006). *Mindset: The new psychology of success*. New York, NY: Ballantine Books.

Education Trust. (2006). *Teaching inequality. How poor and minority students are shortchanged on teacher quality*. Washington, DC: Author.

Eisenberg, D., & Neighbors, K. (2007). *Economics of preventing mental disorders and substance abuse among young people*. Paper commissioned by the Committee on Prevention of Mental Disorders and Substance Abuse Among Children, Youth, and Young Adults: Research Advances and Promising Interventions, Board on Children, Youth, and Families. National Research Council and Institute of Medicine, Washington, DC.

Eisenberger, N., & Lieberman, M. (2004). Why rejection hurts: a common neural alarm system for physical and social pain. *Trends in Cognitive Sciences*, *8*(7), 294–300.

Gentile, D., & Bushman, B. (2012). Reassessing media violence effects using a risk and resilience approach to understanding aggression. *Psychology of Popular Media Culture*, *1*(3), 138–151. doi:10.1037/a0028481

Gerhardt, S. (2004). *Why love matters: How affection shapes a baby's brain*. London, UK: Brunner Routledge.

Gerhardt, S. (2015). *Why love matters: How affection shapes a baby's brain*. London, UK: Brunner Rutledge.

Government of British Columbia Ministry of Education. (2018). BC's new curriculum. Retrieved from https://curriculum.gov.bc.ca/

Gray, P. (2013). *Free to learn*. New York, NY: Basic Books.

Groos, K. (1898). *The play of animals*. New York, NY: Appleton.

Hammond, Z. (2015). *Culturally responsive teaching and the brain: Promoting authentic engagement and rigor among culturally and liguistically diverse students*. Thousand Oaks, CA: Corwin.

Harvard Health Publishing. (2018). Anxiety and physical illness: Understanding and treating anxiety can often improve the outcome of chronic disease, such as GI tract problems and heart disease. Retrieved from https://www.health.harvard.edu/staying-healthy/anxiety_and_physical_illness

Hofstede, G., Hofstede, G. J., & Minkov, M. (2010). *Cultures and organizations: Software of the mind*. New York, NY: Mcgraw-Hill.

Howard-Jones, P., Taylor, J., & Sutton, L. (2002). The effect of play on the creativity of young children during subsequent activity. *Early Child Development and Care, 172*(4), 323–328.

ICD-11. (n.d.). Disorders due to addictive behaviors. Retrieved from https://icd.who.int/dev11/l-m/en#/http%3a%2f%2fid.who.int%2ficd%2fentity%2f499894965

Jung, C. (1966). *The spirit in man, art, and literature*. Princeton, NJ: Princeton University Press.

Kalyanpur, M., & Harry, B. (2012). *Cultural reciprocity in special education: Building family-professional relationships*. Baltimore, MD: Paul H. Brooks.

Kennedy, S. E., Koeppe, R. A., Young, E. A., & Zubieta, J. K. (2006). Dysregulation of endogenous opiod emotion regulation circuitry in major depression in women. *Archives of General Psychiatry, 63*(11), 1199–1208.

Klem, A., & Conell, J. P. (2004). Relationships matter: Linking teacher support to student engagement and achievement. *Journal of School Health, 74*(7), 262–273.

Koob, G. E. (2008). A role for brain stress systems in addiction. *Neuron, 59*(1), 11–34.

Kuss, D. J., & Griffiths, M. D. (2011). Excessive online social networking: Can adolescents become addicted to Facebook? *Education and Health, 29*(4), 68–71.

Lee, R. (1988). Reflections on primitive communism. In D. Riches, J. Woodburn, & T. Ingold (Eds.), *Hunters and gatherers* (pp. 252–268). Oxford, UK: Berg.

Lieberman, D. E. (2013). *The story of the human body*. New York, NY: Vintage Books.

Mate, G. (2012). Addiction: Childhood trauma, stress and the biology of addiction. *Journal of Restorative Medicine, 1*(1), 56–63.

Means, B., & Knapp, M. S. (1991). Rethinking teaching for disadvantaged students. In B. Means, C. Chelemer, & M. S. Knapp (Eds.), *Teaching advanced skills to at-risk students: Views from research and practice* (pp. 1–26). San Francisco, CA: Jossey-Bass.

Merikangas, R. (2010). Prevalence and treatment of mental disorders among U.S. children in the 2001–2004 NHANES. *Pediatrics, 125*(1), 75–81.

Mitra, S. (2003). Minimally invasive education: A progress report on the "hole-in-the-wall" experiments. *British Journal of Educational Technology, 34*(3), 367–371.

Mojtabai, R., Olfson, M., & Han, B. (2016). National trends in the treatment of depression in adolescents and young adults. *Pediatrics*, *138*(6), e20161878.

Montgomery, J., & Ritchey, T. (2008). *The answer model theory*. Santa Monica, CA: TAM Books.

Montgomery, J., & Ritchey, T. (2010). *Answer model: A new path to healing*. Santa Monica, CA: TAM Books.

National Institute of Mental Health. (2005). Prevalence of any anxiety disorder among adolescents. Retrieved from http://www.nimh.nih.gov/health/statistics/any-anxiety-disorder.shtml

Panksepp, J. (2014, January 13). *The science of emotions at TEDxRanier*. Seattle, WA: TEDx.

Panksepp, J. (n.d.). About [Facebook]. Retreived from https://www.facebook.com/pages/Jaak-Panksepp/124170027627971

Pert, C. B., & Snyder, S. H. (1973). Opiate receptor: Demonstration in nervous tissue. *Science*, *179*(4077), 1011–1014.

Pruessner, J., Champagne, F., Meaney, M. J., & Dagher, A. (2004). Dopamine release in response to a psychological stress in humans and its relationship to early life maternal care. *Journal of Neuroscience*, *24*(11), 2825–2831.

Przybyski, A. K., Weinstein, N., Ryan, R., & Rigby, C. S. (2009). Having versus wanting to play: Background and consequences of harmonious versus obsessive engagement in video games. *Cyberpsychology & Behavior*, *12*, 485–492.

Redfield, J. (1994). *The Celestine Prophesy*. London, UK: Bantam Books.

Rideout V.J., Foehr, U.G., & Roberts, D.F. (2010, January) *Generation M²: Media in the lives of 8- to 18-year-olds*. Menlo Park, CA: The Henry J. Kaiser Family Foundation. Retrieved from https://files.eric.ed.gov/fulltext/ED527859.pdf

Robinson, T., & Berridge, K. (2016). Liking, wanting, and the incentive-sensitization theory of addiction. *American Psychologist*, *71*(8), 670–679.

Rowan, C. (2010). Unplug—Don't drug: A critical look at the influence of technology on child behavior with an alternative way of responding other than evaluation and drugging. *Ethical Human Psychology and Psychiatry*, *12*(1), 60–68.

Santa Barbara Graduate Institute Center for Clinical Studies and Research. (n.d.). Trauma, Attachment, and Stress Disorders: Rethinking and Reworking Developmental Issues. *HealingResources.info*. Retrieved from http://www.healingresources.info/trauma_attachment_stress_disorders.html

Shaffer, H. J. (2017). *Overcoming addiction: Paths toward recovery*. Harvard Medical School Special Health Report. Boston, MA: Harvard Health Publishing.

Twenge, J. (2011). Generational differences in mental health: Are children and adolescents suffering more or less? *American Journal of Orthopsychiatry*, *81*(4), 469–472.

Twenge, J., Zhang, L., & Im, C. (n.d.). It's beyond my control: A cross-temporal meta-analysis of increasing externality in locus of control, 1960–2002. *Personality and Social Psychology Review*, *8*(3), 308–319.

Visser, S. N., Danielson, M. L., Bitsko, R. H., Holbrook, J. R., Kogan, M. D., Ghandour, R, M., … Blumberg, S. J. (2014). Trends in the Parent Report of Health Care Provideri Diagnosed and Medicated ADHD US 2003–2011. *Journal of the American Academy of Child and Adolescent Pscychiatry*, *53*(1), 34–46.

Volpicelli, J., Balaraman, G., Hahn, J., Wallace, H., & Bux, D. (1999). The role of uncontrollable trauma in the development of PTSD and alcohol addiction. *Alcohol Research and Health*, *23*(4), 256–262.

Vygotsky, L. S. (1978). *Mind in society: The development of higher psychological processes.* Cambridge, MA: Harvard University Press.

Whiting, B. B. (1983). The genesis of prosocial behavior. In D. L. Bridgeman (Ed.), *The nature of prosocial development: Interdisciplinarytheories and strategies* (pp. 221–242). New York, NY: Academic Press.

Wilcox, E. (1999). Straight talk about music and brain research. *Teaching Music, 7*(3), 29, 31–35.

Wright, R. (1994). *The moral animal.* New York, NY: Vintage.

Yeager, D. S., Bundick, M. J., & Johnson, R. (2012). The role of future work goal motives in adolescent identity development: A longitudinal mixed-methods investigation. *Contempory Educational Psychology, 37*(3), 206–217.

Index

Brain
    emotions and, 3, 46
    feeding Good Wolf and, 24
    neural network patterns, 46
    resiliency of, 48
    training, 49
Brain development, 2, 47, 48
Bravery, 183. *See also* Challenge
Bullying, 83, 156

Case studies
    embracing uncomfortable, 53
    multi-grade learning environments, 117–118
    peer connections, 115–116
    setting intentions, 38–39
    unit plans, 150–153
    using games, 25–26
Challenge, 35–36, 52, 102–104, 183
    limiting, 54–55
    physical, 100–102
    ultra-safety and, 64
    See also Discomfort
Change, 9, 50–52. *See also* Challenge; Growth
Cheerleading, enthusiastic, 39–40
Choice
    authentic, 163–164
    behaviors as, 161–164, 163 (fig)
Classroom
    connection in, 22–23. *See also* Emotionally
        Connected Classroom model
    hunter-gatherer theme in, 18–19
    See also Behavior management; Education;
        Learning; School; Structure
Closure, in lesson plans, 148–150
Coaching, 49, 177
Comey, James, 28
Communication, transmission of knowledge and, 17
Competitive school environments, 124, 127
Compliment skills, 40
Connectedness, 22. *See also* Beliefs, authentic
Connection
    academic achievement and, 21
    authentic, 1
    baby steps in connection, 96–98, 148
    brain development and, 4
    definitions of, 21–22
    effects of, 22
    healthy, 3
    importance of, 7
    nurturing, 18–19
    physiological response to, 10
    rewards and, 33
    transmission of knowledge and, 17
Connection checklist, 97, 97 (fig)
Connection intentions, 24, 37, 50, 56
    aligning education with, 40–41
    assessing, 40–41
    culturally responsive, 68
    as diagnostic tool for emotional wellness, 37–38
    effective, 23
    example, 132

feeding Good Wolf and, 25
goals of, 40
implementing, 94–106
measuring, 148–150
selecting, 36–39
setting, 23–25
targets in, 145
See also Interventions; Lesson plans; Planning
    connection intentions; Six Ps of Connection
Connection skills, 96
    being cheerleader for, 39–40
    modeling, 145
    for multi-grade learning environments, 119
    nurturing, 12
    pulling together, 143
Connection standards, 145–146
Content objectives. *See* Curriculum
Contributing, 12–13, 29, 115, 175–176
Control
    behavior and, 156
    of education, 66
    of environment, 124
    loss of, 61
    sense of, 62
    of thinking/feeling, 33
Control dramas, 156–159, 157 (fig), 163, 164
Control strategies. *See* Behavior management
Cooperation, play and, 178
Coping strategies, 15–16, 72. *See also* Survival mode
Cortisol, 10, 77
Crash, 80–81
Creativity, play and, 178
Cultural disconnections in education, 66–68
Culturally responsive education, 67–68
Culturally Responsive Teaching and the Brain
    (Hammond), 67
Cultural transmission, 17, 66
Curriculum, 6, 40
    connection-based, 23–24
    content-based, 141
    See also Content objectives; Learning outcomes

Deadlines, 128
Depression, 14, 48, 59. *See also* Mental health issues
Difference, valuing, 179
Discomfort, 5, 35, 49, 52, 53, 100–102, 143, 165,
    182–183. *See also* Challenge
Disconnecting pressures, 60, 61, 73
Disconnection, 9, 59
    ability to learn and, 15
    definition of, 22
    education and, 6
    effects of, 14, 93
    health and, 59
    media technology and, 68–70
    modern-day, 60
    from natural learning instincts, 17–18
    See also Anxiety; Survival mode
Dopamine, 10, 77, 78, 80. *See also* Stress hormones
Drama, emotional, 155–159. *See also* Control dramas
Dweck, Carol, 24, 50

Pleasing people, 166–168
Poor Me personality, 156–159, 160
Posture, engaged, 39
Present thinking, 33–35, 98–102, 126, 127, 180–181.
    See also Six Ps of Connection
Procrastination, chronic, 81–82, 83
Protection, 54, 126
Protection-avoidance strategies, 54, 55 (fig)
Purpose, 29–30, 95–98, 175–177. *See also* Six Ps of
    Connection

Ready for Rigor Framework, 68 (fig)
Reality, beliefs as, 124–125
Reflection, 147–150
Resiliency, 47, 72, 99, 100, 178, 183
Responsibility, 29–30, 178
Rewards, 3
    of addictive drive, 75
    authentic, 1, 63
    connection and, 33
    extrinsic, 61
    intrinsic, 61
    passions and, 63
    See also Payoffs
Risk, 35, 54–55, 64. *See also* Challenge
Ritchey, Todd, 5
Romeo and Juliet (Shakespeare), 38–39, 50, 185
Rules, 156, 159–160

Safety
    anxiety and, 124–125
    communal, 174–175
    control of, 123
    early attachments and, 47–48
    feelings of, 123–126
    promises of, 125
    protection, 126
    responsibility for, 125–126, 134
    risk and, 64
    self-esteem and, 64–65
    sense of, 22
    Statement of Safety, 99, 126, 142
Safety attachments, cultural obsession with, 54–55
School
    compared to natural learning, 18
    competitive environments in, 124, 127
    emotional safety/wellness and, 47–48
    freeze response in, 16
    See also Classroom; Education; Learning
Screen time, 48. *See also* Media technology
Self, sense of, 60, 63. *See also* True self
Self-assessment, formative, 149
Self-beliefs, false, 51. *See also* False-self stories
Self-esteem, 54, 64–65
Self-worth, 12–13, 22, 29, 69
Separation anxiety, 53
Shakespeare, William, 38–39, 50
Sink-or-swim approach, 55, 55 (fig)
Six Ps of Connection, 6, 21, 27–35, 50
    connection intentions and, 173–183
    implementing purposeful intentions, 94–106

in lesson plans, 141–142
One-Two-Three connection intervention,
    95–106
passions, 31, 63, 95–98, 179
people, connections with, 28–29, 95–98, 173–175
personal challenge, 35–36, 52, 54–55, 64, 102–104,
    183. *See also* Discomfort
personal growth, 182–183
play, 30–31, 95–98, 178–179
present thinking, 33–35, 98–102, 126, 127,
    180–181
purpose, 29–30, 95–98, 175–177
selecting, 36–37
See also Connection intentions; Planning
    connection intentions
Skills, connection. *See* Connection skills
Skills, twenty-first century, 6
Smart phones. *See* Media technology
Snyder, Solomon, 78
Social, being, 174
Social conditions, stress and, 13–14
Socialization, transmission of knowledge and, 17
Social media. *See* Media technology
Sports
    emotions and, 49
    See also PE (physical education)
Standards, connection, 145–146
Statement of Safety, 99, 126, 142
Status, 12–13, 158
Stress
    health and, 82 (fig)
    learning and, 6
    modern-day, 13–14
    parent relationships and, 77
    as precursor for addiction, 77
    unnecessary, 103–104, 130
    See also Trauma
Stress hormones, 4, 10, 77. *See also* Dopamine;
    Endorphins
Stressors, status-driven, 13
Structure, 127, 134 (fig)
    authentic, 127, 132, 133
    cooperative, 127
    dynamic, 134–136
    five-step daily structure, 133
    in lesson plans, 144–146
    play learning and, 132–133
    role of in anxiety intervention, 132–136
Struggle, 64–65. *See also* Challenge; Failure
Student-centered classroom, 30
Students of color, 66–68
Student–teacher control dramas, 157–158
Student–teacher relationships, 111–112
Success, communal, 174
Suicide, 14. *See also* Mental health issues
Support groups, educated, 110–111
Survival mode, 4, 10–11, 12, 13, 15–17, 79. *See also*
    Avoidance; Disconnection

Talents. *See* Passions
Targets, connection. *See* Intentions

A SAGE Publishing Company

Helping educators make the greatest impact

CORWIN HAS ONE MISSION: to enhance education through intentional professional learning. We build long-term relationships with our authors, educators, clients, and associations who partner with us to develop and continuously improve the best evidence-based practices that establish and support lifelong learning.

Solutions YOU WANT | Experts YOU TRUST | Results YOU NEED

EVENTS

>>> **INSTITUTES**

Corwin Institutes provide large regional events where educators collaborate with peers and learn from industry experts. Prepare to be recharged and motivated!

corwin.com/institutes

ON-SITE PD

>>> **ON-SITE PROFESSIONAL LEARNING**

Corwin on-site PD is delivered through high-energy keynotes, practical workshops, and custom coaching services designed to support knowledge development and implementation.

corwin.com/pd

>>> **PROFESSIONAL DEVELOPMENT RESOURCE CENTER**

The PD Resource Center provides school and district PD facilitators with the tools and resources needed to deliver effective PD.

corwin.com/pdrc

ONLINE

>>> **ADVANCE**

Designed for K–12 teachers, Advance offers a range of online learning options that can qualify for graduate-level credit and apply toward license renewal.

corwin.com/advance

Contact a PD Advisor at (800) 831-6640 or
visit www.corwin.com for more information

CORWIN